Bias Square
Miniatures

Christine Carlson

That Patchwork Place®

CREDITS

Editor-in-Chief .... Barbara Weiland
Technical Editor .... Christine Barnes
Managing Editor ....Greg Sharp
Illustrators .... Brian Metz
Laurel Strand
Illustration Assistant .... Lisa McKenney
Cover Designer .... Judy Petry
Text Designer .... Kay Green
Design Assistant .... Shean Bemis
Copy Editor .... Tina Cook
Proofreader .... Leslie Phillips
Photographer ....Brent Kane

Bias Square® Miniatures
©1995 by Christine Carlson

That Patchwork Place, Inc.
PO Box 118, Bothell, WA 98041-0118 USA

Printed in the United States of America
00 98 97 96 95   6 5 4 3 2 1

Library of Congress Cataloging-in-Publication Data
Carlson, Christine,
Bias square miniatures / Christine Carlson.
p.   cm.
IBSN 1–56477–099–0 (pbk.)
1. Quilting—Patterns.   2. Patchwork—Patterns.
3. Miniature quilts.   I. Title.
TT835.C373   1995
746.46'0228—dc20   95-894
CIP

Mission Statement

WE ARE DEDICATED TO PROVIDING QUALITY PRODUCTS THAT ENCOURAGE CREATIVITY AND PROMOTE SELF-ESTEEM IN OUR CUSTOMERS AND OUR EMPLOYEES.

WE STRIVE TO MAKE A DIFFERENCE IN THE LIVES WE TOUCH.

That Patchwork Place is an employee-owned, financially secure company.

ACKNOWLEDGMENTS

I extend special thanks to wonderful friends:

Marianne Webb, who, in spite of her busy schedule, tested patterns and quickly organized an accomplished group of pattern testers in the Atlanta area;

Marianne Burrows, Paula Heiney, Susan Kent, and Kathy Niemann, for their excited responses to my call for help and their beautiful test quilts;

My best friend, Brian Prazich, whose help and support behind the scenes enabled me to do what I needed to do without feeling guilty;

Sandra Hatch, Editor, House of White Birches magazines, who gave me my first big break in the publishing world;

The Georgia quilt shops that helped me find pattern testers: Calico Quilters, Roswell; Dream Quilters, Tucker; Tiny Stitches, Marietta; and The Village Quilt Shop, Stone Mountain;

My wonderful children, Marcia and Daniel, who encourage me in my quilting and writing and praise my accomplishments;

Christine Barnes, who patiently and painstakingly edited my manuscript, offering guidance and support along the way;

Ursula Reikes and Marion Shelton at That Patchwork Place, who helped me get started and graciously answered my questions;

And, finally, Barbara Weiland, Editor-in-Chief at That Patchwork Place, warm and special thanks for making it all possible.

DEDICATION

To my beautiful granddaughter, Cortney Michelle Roberts, who loves to watch me quilt. I hope that she will become a quilter someday and have as much passion for this fulfilling experience as I do.

Contents

Tiny Treasures

"What exactly is a miniature quilt?" I'm often asked that question by curious quiltmakers and admirers alike. Strictly speaking, a miniature quilt replicates a full-size quilt on a reduced scale, capturing the essence and maintaining the elements of the source quilt. You sometimes hear the terms "miniature" and "small" quilt used interchangeably, although miniature quilts are generally smaller. At most miniature quilt shows, a miniature block may be up to three inches, and a miniature quilt may be up to twenty-four inches on a side.

It's not only size, however, that makes a quilt a miniature. To be considered a true miniature, a quilt must possess a complexity in design and construction that draws "oohs" and "aahs" from quilt enthusiasts. These microquilts are every bit as sophisticated as their full-size counterparts. In fact, miniature quilts are becoming smaller and more complex, with intricate piecing, appliqué, and quilting the rule.

The appeal of these little quilts is tied to the enormous and ever-increasing popularity of all kinds of quilts. Long considered pieces of history and works of art, full-size antique and traditional quilts command high prices. As collectors, antique dealers, and museums buy these quilts, they become scarce—and out of reach for most of us. In response, many quiltmakers have turned to miniatures, which also have roots in history. Years ago, little girls learned to quilt by making doll quilts from their mothers' quilt scraps. These precious doll quilts, many of which survive today, have sparked renewed interest in small-scale scrap quilts.

Quiltmakers love miniatures for practical reasons too. Tiny quilts are relatively inexpensive to make because they require small amounts of fabric. You can live every quilter's dream, buying many different fabrics while spending very little. And you're likely to receive windfalls of scraps from your quilting friends.

Miniatures are portable, allowing you to stitch wherever you go. They are also much less time-consuming than full-size quilts, a real plus for those of us who know we will never have the time or energy to make all the full-size quilts we would love to possess. Making miniatures satisfies our desire to try out a variety of quilt patterns, and we see the fruits of our labor quickly.

Finally, making miniatures is addictive. As soon as I've finished one of these charming little quilts, my mind and fingers are racing to start another. It's not unusual for me to have a number of quilts going at one time. Each pattern presents its own challenges, and with challenge I grow as a quiltmaker and find new satisfaction in my work.

If you've never made a miniature quilt, there's a whole world awaiting you. Take the time to learn (or brush up on) a few techniques, choose a pattern, and search for the perfect fabrics. Then sit down and begin to stitch your own tiny treasure.

About This Book

Where would we be without bias squares? It may sound like a silly question, but if you've been quilting for more than a few years, you probably remember the traditional way of cutting individual triangles and reassembling them to create seamed squares. This method was time-consuming and often inaccurate, especially when joining tiny triangles for a miniature quilt.

Happily, things have changed in the quiltmaking world. With the advent of rotary cutting, resourceful quiltmakers developed speedy methods for cutting and piecing full-size quilts. Making bias squares is an excellent example of a rotary-cutting technique that adapts beautifully to miniatures. With this method, you join two strips of bias-cut fabric, press the seam open, and cut pieced squares using the 4" Baby Bias Square®. (See "Making Bias Squares" on pages 13–17.) The sides of the bias squares are on the straight grain, which prevents them from stretching as you construct the blocks. It couldn't be simpler—or more accurate. If you've never used this technique, you'll be amazed at the results.

Making bias squares for miniatures is the focus of this book, but you'll find much more in these pages. For help in creating a color scheme and buying and preparing fabrics, see "Getting Started." This chapter also includes a discussion of the tools you'll need to create miniature quilts.

"Quiltmaking Basics" takes you through the quiltmaking process, from cutting bias squares to setting blocks and adding borders. Read this important chapter to get a feel for how a miniature quilt is constructed. Many of the techniques are the same as those used to make full-size quilts, but some are geared just to miniatures. The technique for "Preserving the Points" on page 22 is especially important. At every stage, strive for precision and accuracy because careful cutting, piecing, and pressing are necessary to achieve near perfection in your quilts. I often remind my students that the most admirable attributes a miniature quiltmaker can have are patience and perseverance.

Next, turn to the "Gallery" of quilts for ideas and inspiration. As you look at the photos, you'll see bias squares used in a variety of traditional patterns, as well as in my original designs. Study the quilts to see if you can determine which principles of color and design are at work. Of special importance are contrast and variety: to clearly see the quilt pattern (and every bias point), each fabric must be distinctly different.

Once you've chosen a miniature project, let the "Quilt Plans" guide you in every step of construction. These projects range from Beginner to Advanced, with most falling into the Beyond Beginner category. I suggest that you start with one of the easier quilts to get a feel for working in miniature. Refer to "Quiltmaking Basics" if you need help.

I hope that you find as much pleasure and satisfaction in stitching miniature quilts as I do. I predict that once you finish your first quilt, you will not be able to resist making many more.

Getting Started

Making a miniature quilt begins with the right tools and appropriate fabrics. Add to these materials a few principles of color and design, and you'll be well on your way to stitching miniatures to cherish.

Choosing Tools and Supplies

Miniature quilts require the same equipment used to create full-size quilts, plus a few tools that are useful for working with small pieces of fabric.

ROTARY TOOLS

The only accurate way to cut fabric for a miniature quilt is with rotary-cutting equipment. These tools ensure precision, which is critical when making miniatures.

ROTARY CUTTERS. Available in three sizes, rotary cutters resemble pizza cutters with a protective shield for the blade.

Rotary cutters have extremely sharp blades. Always cut with the blade moving away from your body, never toward it. Whenever the cutter is not in use, snap the safety shield over the blade to prevent injury. Carefully dispose of a used blade by wrapping it generously with heavy paper.

ROTARY RULERS. Rotary rulers come in different sizes and grid formats. I prefer Omnigrid® rulers for most measuring and cutting because they are marked for right- and left-handed quilters, and their ⅛" yellow lines are visible on both light and dark fabrics. The 4" square ruler is handy for cutting squares, rectangles, and squaring up blocks, and the 3" x 18" ruler is just the right size for cutting strips. I also use the 1" x 6" ruler for measuring.

A 4" Baby Bias Square is indispensable for making accurate bias square miniatures. The ⅛" markings and diagonal line are designed for cutting small bias squares. A 6" Bias Square is also helpful when aligning your rotary ruler for the first cut on a piece of fabric.

CUTTING MATS. A self-healing rotary-cutting mat holds the fabric in place and protects both the blade and the work surface. Mats come in various sizes and with different markings.

To preserve the mat, hold the rotary cutter with the blade perpendicular to the ruler. Keep rotary mats away from heat and cold.

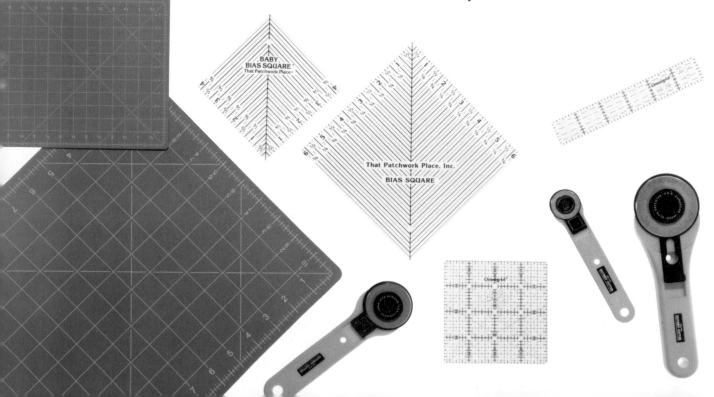

SEWING TOOLS

SEWING MACHINE. Any straight-stitch sewing machine is suitable for making miniatures. A straight-stitch throat plate, with its small, round opening, helps prevent the fabric from being "eaten" when you begin a seam.

For miniatures, I prefer my vintage Singer® Featherweight because it produces a fine stitch and has a small presser foot with ¼" and ⅛" seam-allowance guides.

SEWING MACHINE NEEDLES. A fine needle produces a fine stitch and is less likely to pull the fabric under the throat plate. I like to use a #60 or #65 needle; use these delicate needles with care because they break easily. My next choice is a #70 needle.

SEWING MACHINE THREAD. A fine, high-quality thread produces fine stitches and allows you to press seams flat. Some quilters use only cotton or cotton-wrapped polyester thread, but I piece with Mettler Metrosene polyester thread because it's very fine.

It is easier to see small machine stitches if the thread is slightly lighter or darker than the quilt fabric. When making a multicolored quilt, I use a neutral color.

QUILTING NEEDLES. The larger the quilting needle number, the finer the needle. I prefer the large-eyed #10 Betweens. The shaft is slender and not too long, and the eye is easy to thread.

HAND QUILTING THREAD. I use Mettler Metrosene polyester thread for hand quilting because it doesn't fray and it comes in a wonderful array of colors.

BASTING THREAD AND PINS. White thread made especially for basting is strong and doesn't tangle. Because I dislike basting with thread, I pin-baste with small brass safety pins.

SCISSORS. The only scissors you need are regular sewing scissors and short scissors with sharp points for trimming seams.

PINS. I use Collins #104 long, straight-head silk pins, which have a fine shaft. Short pins or large pins with glass heads just aren't right for miniature quiltmaking.

SEAM RIPPER. Even the best sewers must remove stitches now and then, and a small seam ripper is an invaluable tool. The point of a large seam ripper is also helpful for guiding small pieces of fabric under the presser foot.

IRONING EQUIPMENT. You'll need an iron and an ironing surface to press the seams. A gridded ironing board cover is helpful when pressing blocks.

SPRAY SIZING. To return the crispness to prewashed fabrics and make cutting and sewing small pieces easier, spray your fabric liberally with sizing.

STORAGE SYSTEM. I place small, cut pieces on paper plates to avoid losing them, then I stack the plates for easy storage. Plastic bags that "zip" shut are also useful for storing pieces.

DRAWING TOOLS. Accurate ¼" or ⅛" (I prefer the smaller grid) graph paper is a must for pattern drafting, along with a C-Thru® plastic ruler, a fine-point mechanical pencil, a good eraser, and tracing paper. Graph paper can vary, so use the same paper throughout a project.

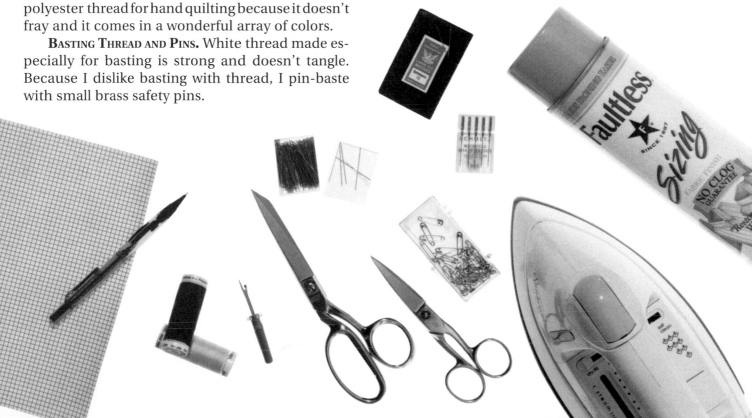

Understanding Color and Design

Selecting the right colors is perhaps the most important step in designing a miniature quilt. Your workmanship may be exquisite, but no one will notice your quilt if the color combination is less than pleasing. To create successful color schemes, consider how color works in miniatures.

COLOR PRINCIPLES

As you think about combining colors in your quilts, keep in mind the following color concepts.

Mood

When choosing colors, ask yourself what mood or feeling you want to evoke. Deep colors set a somber mood, while dreamy pastels create a feminine feeling. Intense colors, such as those in "Lawyer's Puzzle" on page 34, often lend a contemporary look to a quilt.

Value

Value refers to the lightness or darkness of color. Without distinctly different values, your eye can't "read" most quilt patterns. Think, for example, of a Log Cabin quilt: you see the block pattern and the setting because some logs are light and others dark. When I plan a scrap quilt, the first thing I do after choosing colors is to divide my scraps into piles of light, medium, and dark values.

Contrast

Good color contrast is essential in miniature quilts. You must create contrast not only within a block but also between the blocks, background, sashing, and borders.

When I choose colors for a quilt that features bias squares, I think first of the points formed by the triangles. Without sharp color contrast between the fabrics, the points blend into the background.

Color contrast also creates dimension in a quilt. The blocks in "Sawtooth Flying Geese" on page 37 create the illusion of depth because the red and blue pieces are set against a white background.

COLOR CUES

To achieve color harmony in a quilt, choose fabrics that are both unified and varied. Needless to say, this process can be daunting. The following guidelines will help you make wise color decisions. See the photos on page 33.

Coordinating Colors

If you're not sure where to begin, try building a color scheme with one or two of your favorite colors. For example, if you want to design a pink-and-blue quilt, pick a light, medium, and dark print of each color for a total of six colors. To make the scheme more interesting, add one or more fabrics that don't quite match the original fabrics.

Avoiding Overmatching

If you select a fabric and try to find others with exactly the same colors, the fabrics may blend so well that the quilt pattern is lost. Close shading works in a large quilt, but not in a miniature.

Planning Scrap Quilts

When I plan a scrap quilt, I almost always include a "zinger" color or two. These colors—red, yellow, and orange—add contrast, movement, and visual interest to a quilt design. When sprinkled throughout a quilt, the eye catches these colors first, then travels to the next bright area. In "Fish School" on page 34, the specks of brilliant orange keep the eye moving across the quilt.

Although I have quilting friends who make true scrap quilts by using every fabric they have on hand, sometimes with dizzying results, this approach does not work with miniatures. Because the pieces are small, a miniature scrap quilt needs a unifying element such as a common color. In "Triangle Puzzle" on page 36, blue is the unifying color.

A COLOR RECIPE

Another approach to color is to choose a quilt theme, such as country or contemporary, and select prints in colors and values that fit the mood. In "Windmill" on page 39, the fabrics are traditional country prints in subdued shades.

Scale

It's best to choose prints in keeping with the small scale of miniature quilts. Sometimes I use a medium-scale print for the borders or backing, or even the blocks. When cut into small pieces, a medium- or large-scale print may fit right in—but you won't know until you try.

Auditioning Fabrics

To see if a fabric will work in a miniature quilt, cut out the appropriate block shape from a piece of white paper. Place the paper window over the fabric to see how it will look as a piece in the block.

It's also helpful to view fabrics from a distance. Arrange your fabrics on a piece of white flannel or foam-core board attached to a wall. Step back to see if the fabrics work well together; they should have good color and value contrast, yet appear harmonious as a group. If you're deliberating between two similar fabrics, always choose the brighter of the two. Quilts with brighter palettes and "color surprises" have greater impact.

Selecting and Preparing Fabric

Shopping for fabrics is for me the most challenging and enjoyable part of planning a miniature quilt. I prepare before I shop by checking my inventory of fabrics to see what I need. The minute I run short of a favorite fabric, I tuck a swatch of it into my purse for future shopping trips.

It's not unusual to end up using fabrics other than those you originally chose. Many times I've bought fabrics that seemed ideal, only to discard some as my ideas evolved. If it's any comfort, the changes are always for the better.

A SHOPPING STRATEGY

Quilters often ask me how I approach fabric selection for my miniatures. Here are answers to a few shopping questions.

- **WHICH COMES FIRST, THE PATTERN OR THE FABRIC?** The answer is, both! However, in most cases, I begin with the quilt pattern and then search for fabrics that fit the mood and style I hope to create. For "Maple Leaf" on page 35, I selected rich prints to represent vibrant fall colors. The classical design of "Grecian" on page 39 suggested vintage fabrics.

- **WHAT KIND OF FABRIC SHOULD I BUY?** Your finished project is only as good as your fabrics, so use top-quality, 100% cotton. Never use polyester blends in your miniature quilts. They look different when placed next to all-cotton fabrics, and they don't "give" as much as cottons, which is important when sewing and pressing small pieces.

- **WHAT KINDS OF PRINTS SHOULD I BUY?** To create texture and visual interest in your quilts, select a variety of prints. Plaids, checks, stripes, pindots, polka dots, paisleys, directional, and allover prints are appropriate.

- **HOW MUCH SHOULD I BUY?** Generally, buy ¼- or ⅓-yard cuts. If I really love a fabric, I'll buy half a yard or a yard. I also buy at least ½-yard cuts if I think the fabric will work as the border or backing, or if I need sashing strips cut on the lengthwise grain. Fat quarters (18" x 22") and half fat quarters (11" x 18") are convenient for cutting bias strips.

Coordinated and Specialty Fabrics

Perhaps you like to browse the bolts at your local quilt shop and make your choices without guidance. You may, however, appreciate a little help from fabric manufacturers and quilt shop owners.

COMPANION FABRICS. I'm always on the lookout for new lines of coordinated fabrics suitable for miniatures. I usually buy at least ¼ yard of each companion fabric, often without a specific quilt in mind.

PRECUT SETS. Quilt shops cut either half–fat quarter or fat-quarter pieces of fabric and sell them as a set, a great help for those who have difficulty coordinating fabrics.

REPRODUCTION PRINTS. The small-scale prints and varied colors in reproduction fabrics make them ideal for miniature quilts. Every chance I get, I add to my collection because I never know when reproduction fabrics will become difficult to find.

VINTAGE FABRICS. I never combine vintage fabrics with new fabrics, even reproduction fabrics, in the same miniature quilt. The colors, designs and patinas of vintage fabrics don't mix well with new fabrics. Even though a quilt made of vintage fabrics is not an antique, it has the look and feel of one.

FABRIC PREPARATION

Preparing your fabrics properly is an important, if unexciting, step in the quiltmaking process. The results are worth the effort, especially when you think of the years of pleasure a quilt brings.

To Prewash or Not?

I don't usually prewash new fabric because I like the look and feel of it. With miniatures, it's also easier to cut and sew fabric that has not been washed. If you choose to prewash your fabric, use a phosphate-free soap to minimize fading.

I do prewash muslin, a loosely woven fabric that can stretch during handling. I wet the muslin and shrink it in the dryer, then use spray sizing to return the crispness. I prewash dark fabrics because they often contain excess dye, which may run when the fabric or quilt is washed, sprayed with sizing, or pressed with a steam iron. I've also found that if I quilt unwashed dark fabrics, excess dyes rub off onto my fingers and onto lighter-colored fabrics in the quilt.

To test for colorfastness, cut a small piece of the fabric and place it in a glass with hot water. If the water changes color, you must prewash the fabric.

Cleaning Soiled or Musty Fabrics

Fabric that is dusty or musty smelling, has spots, or is soiled must be properly cleaned before cutting and sewing. Soil and dust break down the fibers in the fabric and cause premature aging. Ironing soiled or spotted fabrics sets the stains.

Pretreat spots and soak the fabric in a mild solution of cold water and Axion® or Bix® overnight; rinse in cold water. Soak dusty or musty fabrics in the bathtub with cold water and Orvus® paste; rinse in cold water.

I have soaked soiled vintage fabric in a solution of cold water and Axion or Orvus with great success, but if you are in doubt about preparing vintage fabric this way, contact a fabric conservation expert.

THE IMPORTANCE OF GRAIN

A piece of fabric has three grain lines. The grain line that runs parallel to the woven selvage is the lengthwise grain; it has very little or no give. The grain line that runs across the fabric from selvage to selvage is the crosswise grain; it has some give. The third grain line, the true bias, runs at a 45° angle to the lengthwise and crosswise grains. Fabric stretches easily on the true bias.

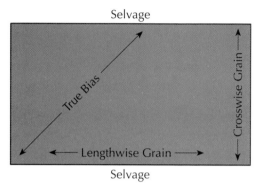

Lengthwise and crosswise grain lines are perpendicular to each other and are both considered to be on the straight grain. Fabric that's been cut off grain may stretch out of shape when sewn and pressed, so it's important to cut it on the straight grain.

If you don't know if the cut edge is on the straight grain, make a small cut at one end and tear a narrow strip to find the grain line.

On an odd-sized piece of fabric, it may be difficult to determine the straight grain. Hold the piece up to the light and look for the grain line on one edge. Make a small cut at one end of this edge and tear a narrow strip. On an adjacent side, repeat this process, resulting in a right-angle corner with both sides on the straight grain.

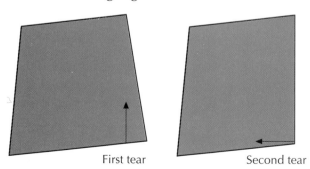

First tear   Second tear

Repeat on the remaining sides. Press the torn edges before you trim them.

Quiltmaking Basics

The tips and techniques in this how-to chapter will guide you in every step of making a miniature quilt. Peruse these pages to get a sense of how a miniature quilt is constructed, then refer to the instructions as you make one of the projects beginning on page 42. You can also use the information presented here to make miniatures of your own design.

Drafting Patterns

Knowing how to draft patterns gives you the freedom to adapt blocks, both full-size and small, for miniature quilts. You can "scale down" a large block or "scale up" a small block. If you enlarge a simple block too much, it will not look like a miniature. Conversely, a complicated block made too small is difficult to sew, and you won't see the individual pieces or the overall pattern.

Pieced patterns can be divided into sections. Some of these divisions are equal, as in a Ninepatch block, while others are unequal, as in a Puss in a Corner block.

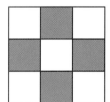

Ninepatch Block
Equal Divisions

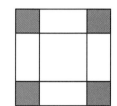

Puss in a Corner Block
Unequal Divisions

Whether you draft up or down, the procedure is the same.

1. Gather the drawing equipment you need. See "Choosing Tools and Supplies" on pages 6–7.
2. Determine the number of divisions in the block and whether these divisions are equal or unequal. Shoo Fly, for example, is a Ninepatch block with 3 equal divisions across and down for a total of 9 divisions or patches.

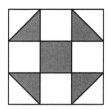

Shoo Fly Block

3. Draw the perimeter of the block to the desired finished size. For easier measuring and cutting, it's best to work with a block size divisible by 1" or ½". Measure and mark the divisions on the new block, maintaining the proportions of the original. Because it contains 3 equal divisions, Shoo Fly reduces easily to 3" blocks (with 1" divisions) or 1½" blocks (with ½" divisions).

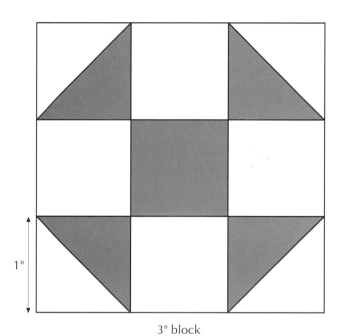

1"

3" block

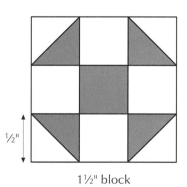

½"

1½" block

Learning to Rotary Cut

Following are instructions for basic rotary cutting of strips, squares, rectangles, bias strips and bias squares, and triangles.

PREPARING THE EDGES

1. Place the fabric on the mat, with the fabric to your left and the ruler to the right; reverse this placement if you are left-handed. Hold the ruler firmly, and steady it by placing your little finger on the table.
2. With the blade perpendicular to the ruler, trim the selvage, rolling the cutter away from you. On a long strip, walk your fingers up the ruler as you cut, maintaining firm pressure.

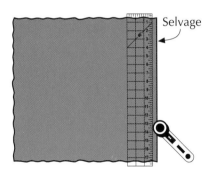
Selvage

3. Turn the cutting mat so that the fabric edge just cut is at the bottom. Align a Bias Square, preferably a 6" x 6" one, with the cut edge. Place a long ruler next to the Bias Square to form a right angle.

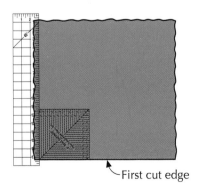
First cut edge

4. Remove the Bias Square and cut along the right edge of the ruler.

You may need to fold your fabric before cutting, but if the fabric isn't folded exactly on grain, the cut edge will be bowed. To avoid this frustration, make a small cut at one end of the fabric and tear a strip to find the straight grain. Press the torn edge.

Fold the fabric in half, matching the torn edges. Align the Bias Square with the fold of the fabric and place the long ruler to the left.

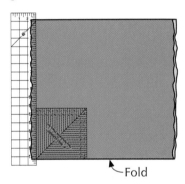
Fold

Remove the Bias Square and cut along the right edge of the ruler to trim the edge.

CUTTING STRIPS

1. Align the vertical ruler markings at the desired width with the clean-cut edge of the fabric; align a horizontal ruler marking with the lower edge of the fabric. After every 3 or 4 cuts, square the cutting edge with the lower edge as in steps 3 and 4 of "Preparing the Edges."

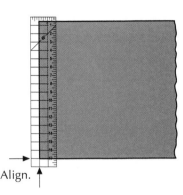
Align.

2. To cut a strip a specific length, align the proper horizontal marking on the ruler with the lower edge of the fabric. Cut the upper edge first so that you won't cut beyond this point when you make the lengthwise cut.

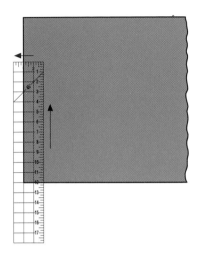

CUTTING SQUARES AND RECTANGLES

For faster cutting of squares, stack two strips.
1. Cut strips equal in width to the measurement of the finished square, plus ½" for seam allowances. Cut the strips 1" longer than needed to allow you to square the cutting edge.
2. Align the Bias Square with the upper and lower edges of the strip; cut squares equal to the width of the strip.

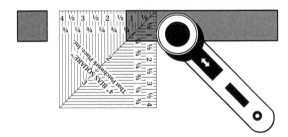

3. Cut rectangles in the same manner. Cut strips equal in width to the measurement of the shorter side of the finished rectangle, plus ½" for seam allowances. Use the longer cut measurement to cut the strips into rectangles.

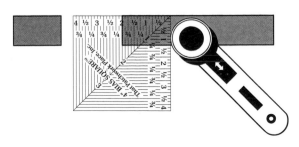

Making Bias Squares

It's essential to cut bias strips on the true bias so that the edges of the bias squares are on the straight grain.

CUTTING BIAS STRIPS

If you cut your fabric pieces to either of two uniform sizes—9" x 18" or 11" x 18"—you can use the bias-square cutting charts on pages 16–17. To cut bias strips from a fat quarter (18" x 22"), it's easiest to first cut the piece into two half–fat quarters, each 11" x 18".

Lay the fabrics, right sides together and raw edges aligned, on your ironing board. Press with a steam iron to make the fabrics adhere to each other; spray the fabrics with sizing.
1. Place the fabrics on the cutting mat with the fabrics to your right and the ruler to your left. If you're left-handed, reverse the directions and use a mirror to look at the illustrations.

2. Align the 45° angle line of your long ruler with the left edge of the fabric and place the upper edge of the ruler at the lower opposite corner of the fabric.

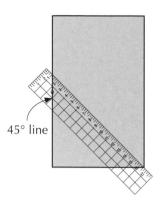

45° line

If you're left-handed, place the lower edge of the ruler at the corner of the fabric.

3. Make the first bias cut along the upper (or lower, if you're left-handed) edge of the ruler. Set aside the 2 lower triangles for cutting additional bias strips if necessary.

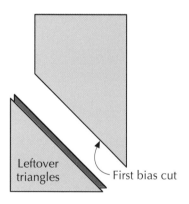

Leftover triangles — First bias cut

4. Align the ruler markings at the desired strip width with the clean-cut edge of the fabric. Make your next bias cut, which will result in two bias strips.

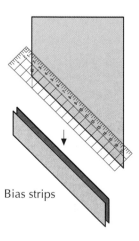

Bias strips

Cutting Narrow Fabric

If your fabric is narrower than 9", don't worry; just cut additional bias strips and lay the fragments end to end and right sides down when pairing them with longer bias strips. When you cut the bias squares, work around the strip fragments.

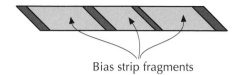

Bias strip fragments

SEWING BIAS STRIPS

Sew the bias strips carefully; if your seam is uneven, your bias squares will not be square.

1. With right sides together and raw edges aligned, stitch the strips, using an accurate ¼"-wide seam allowance. See "Making an Accurate Seam Guide" on page 20. Use a short stitch (16 to 18 stitches per inch) to prevent the stitches from coming undone when you cut the squares. Lengthen the stitch slightly if the stitches pull or the strip doesn't lie flat.

   The seamed strips are referred to as a bias set. One end of the bias set will form a point that is a 90° angle, and the other end will be in the shape of a V.

90° angle   V shape

2. If necessary, cut additional bias strips from the two leftover triangles.

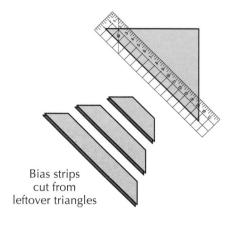

Bias strips cut from leftover triangles

All bias sets made from leftover triangles will form a 90˚ angle at each end.

90° angle

3. Place the bias set wrong side up on the ironing board and gently press the seam open, running your index finger down the seam line as you go. Avoid pressing the bias edges because they stretch out of shape easily.
4. Turn the set right side up and gently press the seam flat, again avoiding the bias edges.

CUTTING BIAS SQUARES

Cut bias squares on point, using the pressed-open seam as your guide for aligning the Baby Bias Square ruler.

1. Lay the bias set wrong side up, with the V shape at the top. With the words "Baby Bias Square" right side up and the numbers upside down, align the 45˚ angle line of the square with the seam.
2. Position the point of the square so that it touches the point of the V. Make 2 cuts along the upper edges of the Bias Square, cutting to the raw edges of the set. The bias set now forms a 90˚ angle at the end.

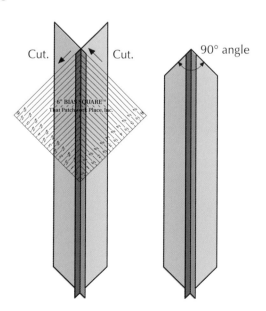

Cut.   Cut.

90° angle

3. Turn the set, maintaining the orientation of the Bias Square. Slide the Bias Square down the set and align the desired bias square measurement with the just-cut edges. Make 2 cuts along the upper edges of the square, cutting to the raw edges of the set to yield 1 bias square.

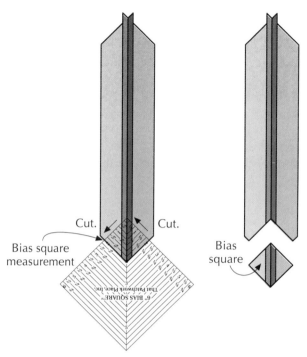

Cut.   Cut.

Bias square measurement

Bias square

4. Continue cutting bias squares from the set in the same manner. Trim the seam allowances of each bias square to ⅛".

If your bias set forms a 90˚ angle at each end, make 2 cuts along the upper edges of the square close to one end to create a perfect angle. Cut the bias squares as instructed in steps 3–4.

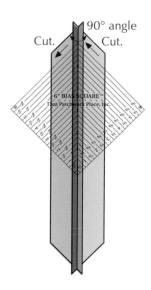

90° angle
Cut.   Cut.

BIAS-SQUARE CUTTING CHARTS

The rule of thumb for cutting bias squares is easy to remember: Start with the desired finished size of the bias square. Add ½" for seam allowances to arrive at the cut size of the bias square. Cut the bias strips the same width as the cut size of the bias squares. If, for example, you want to make a bias square that's 1" finished, cut 1½"-wide bias strips and 1½" bias squares.

The trick is knowing how long the strips must be and how many strips to cut for the number of bias squares needed. To help you quickly determine the strip length and number, refer to the following bias-square cutting charts, labeled A, B, and C.

Cutting Chart A

This chart tells you at a glance how long the bias strip must be to cut one bias square of a certain size.

The strip length is equal to the diagonal measurement, point to point, of the cut bias square. If, for example, you want to make bias squares that are 1" finished, the cut size of each bias square is 1½", and the diagonal measurement is 2⅛". If you require six bias squares, each 1½", you must cut and seam two bias strips, each 1½" wide x 12¾" long (2⅛" x 6 = 12¾"). If possible, cut the bias strips a little longer than necessary in case you miscut.

CUTTING CHART A		
Finished size of bias square:	Cut size of bias square:	Cut length of bias strip:
½"	1"	1½"
⅝"	1⅛"	1⅝"
¾"	1¼"	1¾"
⅞"	1⅜"	2"
1"	1½"	2⅛"
1⅛"	1⅝"	2⅜"
1¼"	1¾"	2½"
1⅜"	1⅞"	2⅝"
1½"	2"	2⅞"
1⅝"	2⅛"	3"
1¾"	2¼"	3¼"
1⅞"	2⅜"	3⅜"
2"	2½"	3½"

Note: The measurements include a ¼"-wide seam allowance.

Cutting Chart B

This chart tells you how many bias squares of a certain finished size you can cut from one bias set. These calculations are based on two pieces of fabric, 9" x 18" or 11" x 18" each, placed right sides together and cut.

The measurements for Chart B are based on cutting the first bias strip as instructed in steps 1–4 on pages 13–14. Remove the leftover triangles and make the subsequent cuts on the remaining fabric.

CUTTING CHART B	
Finished size of bias square:	Number of bias squares that can be cut from a 12½"-long bias set, based on 9" x 18" fabric:
½"	8
⅝"	7
¾"	7
⅞"	6
1"	5
1⅛"	5
1¼"	5
1⅜"	4
1½"	4
1⅝"	4
1¾"	3
1⅞"	3
2"	3
Finished size of bias square:	Number of bias squares that can be cut from a 15½"-long bias set, based on 11" x 18" fabric:
½"	10
⅝"	9
¾"	8
⅞"	7
1"	7
1⅛"	6
1¼"	6
1⅜"	5
1½"	5
1⅝"	5
1¾"	4
1⅞"	4
2"	4

Note: The measurements include a ¼"-wide seam allowance.

Cutting Chart C

This chart tells you how many bias strips you can cut from a 9" x 18" piece of fabric or an 11" x 18" piece of fabric for bias squares of different finished sizes.

CUTTING CHART C		
Finished size of bias square:	**Number of bias strips that can be cut from 9" x 18" piece of fabric:**	**Number of bias strips that can be cut from 11" x 18" piece of fabric:**
½"	6	4
⅝"	5	4
¾"	5	4
⅞"	4	3
1"	4	3
1⅛"	3	2
1¼"	3	2
1⅜"	3	2
1½"	3	2
1⅝"	3	2
1¾"	2	2
1⅞"	2	2
2"	2	2

Note: The measurements include a ¼"-wide seam allowance.

Making Quick-Cut Triangles

When you set quilt blocks on point and sew them into diagonal rows, you need setting triangles to fill in the triangular spaces created by the blocks and plain squares to separate the pieced blocks. (See "Hourglass" on page 38.)

Many of the quilts in this book are set diagonally, and you'll find specific instructions for cutting side and corner setting triangles in the quilt plans. The following instructions will guide you in drafting diagonally set quilt patterns.

What are half-square and quarter-square triangles? As the name implies, these triangles are cut from squares. When you cut a square once diagonally, you create two half-square triangles. Half-square triangles are used at the corners of a diagonally set quilt. When you cut a square twice diagonally, you create four quarter-square triangles. Quarter-square triangles are used at the sides of a quilt.

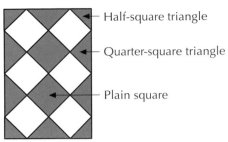

CUTTING HALF-SQUARE TRIANGLES

On a half-square triangle, the long edge of the triangle is on the bias, and the short edges are on the straight grain.

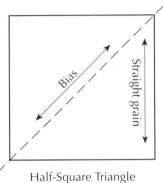

Half-Square Triangle

When you sew these triangles to the quilt corners, the short edges become the outer edges of the quilt top.

To cut half-square triangles, cut a square ⅞" larger than the finished length of the short edge of the triangle. If, for example, the finished length of the short edge of the triangle is 1½", the cut square must measure 2⅜" (1½" + ⅞" = 2⅜"). The ⅞" is the result of adding ⅝" for the seam allowance at the tip of the triangle and ¼" for the seam allowance on the straight edge of the triangle.

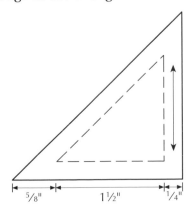

If you don't know the finished length of one short edge of the triangle, it's easiest to refer to Cutting Chart D at right.

CUTTING QUARTER-SQUARE TRIANGLES

On a quarter-square triangle, each short edge is on the bias, and the long edge is on the straight grain.

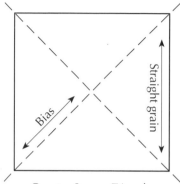

Quarter-Square Triangle

When you sew these triangles to the blocks, the long edges become the outer edges of the quilt top. Because the long edge is on the straight grain, the edges of the quilt will not stretch.

To cut quarter-square triangles, cut a square 1¼" larger than the finished length of the long edge of the triangle. If, for example, the finished length of the long edge of the triangle is 2⅞", the cut square must measure 4⅛" (2⅞" + 1¼" = 4⅛"). The 1¼" is the result of adding ⅝" twice for the seam allowance at each point of the triangle base.

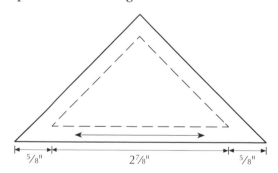

⅝"   2⅞"   ⅝"

If you don't know the finished measurement of the long edge of the triangle, it's easiest to refer to Cutting Chart D above right.

Hint: *If the measurements of the short and long edges of triangles are not even numbers, it's best to round them up to the next ⅛". The triangles will be a bit larger than needed, but you can trim the excess fabric when you square the quilt top.*

Cutting Chart D

Begin with the finished size of the diagonally set blocks in your quilt. Find the finished block size in the first column, then see the second column for the size of the squares needed to cut the half-square corner setting triangles. See the third column for the size of the squares needed to cut the quarter-square side setting triangles.

CUTTING CHART D		
Finished size of block:	**Half-square triangles** Cut size of square:	**Quarter-square triangles** Cut size of square:
½"	1¼"	2"
1"	1⅝"	2¾"
1¼"	1¾"	3"
1½"	2"	3⅜"
1¾"	2⅛"	3¾"
2"	2⅜"	4⅛"
2¼"	2½"	4½"
2½"	2⅝"	4¾"
2¾"	2⅞"	5⅛"
3"	3"	5½"
3¼"	3¼"	5⅞"
3½"	3⅜"	6¼"
3¾"	3⅝"	6⅝"
4"	3¾"	6⅞"

Note: The measurements include a ¼"-wide seam allowance.

For finished blocks that are between the sizes in the chart, use the next larger block size and trim the excess triangle fabric when you square the quilt top, maintaining the ¼"-wide seam allowance and a 90° angle at each corner.

CUTTING OVERSIZED TRIANGLES FOR FLOATING BLOCKS

Diagonally set blocks "float" when their points don't meet the border seams.

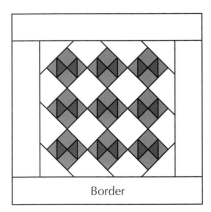

Border

Floating Blocks

To achieve this effect, cut the squares for the corner and side setting triangles at least ½" larger than necessary. Trim the excess fabric at the edges after you join the blocks and triangles, maintaining the ¼"-wide seam allowance. If you are unsure of the square size, experiment with graph paper before cutting the fabric squares.

Mastering Sewing Techniques

It's important to use good sewing techniques with miniature quilts. I measure my blocks at every step, making corrections as needed. Correcting blocks as I go saves me much time and frustration.

SEWING HINTS

Keep your sewing machine performing at its peak. Oil it regularly and remove the lint that accumulates around the bobbin and the feed dogs.

For piecing units or attaching borders, 12 to 14 stitches per inch are usually sufficient. However, to prevent stitches from coming undone when you cut segments or bias squares, you need 16 to 18 stitches per inch for strip piecing and sewing bias strips.

Before starting a project, wind several bobbins so you won't need to stop to re-wind. Use the same thread in the bobbin as on top, since threads of different thicknesses can cause tension problems.

To prevent the sewing machine needle from "eating" your fabric when you start a seam, pull the two sewing threads away from the needle, to the back. Make sure the needle goes through the fabric for several stitches before you let go of the threads.

MAKING AN ACCURATE SEAM GUIDE

It's essential—absolutely essential—to sew a consistent, accurate ¼"-wide seam. Being even a little off "here and there" quickly adds up and affects the finished measurements.

My favorite seam guide consists of a strip of adhesive-backed foam shoe padding, often referred to as "mole foam." The thickness of the foam acts as a ridge that maintains a uniform seam allowance.

1. To position the strip exactly ¼" to the right of the needle, carefully cut out a 2" x 11" piece of ¼"-grid graph paper on the lines. Make sure to cut the right-hand edge precisely on the grid line. With no thread in the needle, carefully lower the needle on the grid line, ¼" from the right edge. Lower the presser foot and sew on the line for several inches.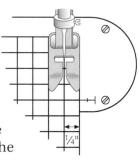

2. Cut a strip of the foam equal in length to the width of your sewing arm. Lay the foam strip next to the cut edge of the graph paper. If the foam covers the feed dogs, mark and cut a notch.

3. Remove the adhesive backing and place the foam strip on the throat plate next to the edge of the paper. Remove the graph paper.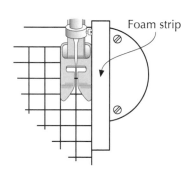

Foam strip

MATCHING SEAMS

For greater accuracy, trim excess bulk at the corners of the seams. You can trim seams pressed to one side and seams pressed open.

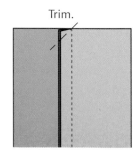
Trim.

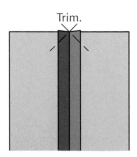
Trim.

To match seams, place the tip of a pin ¼" from the upper raw edge of the pieces, straight through both seams. Pull on the pin to match the seams. This technique will cause the seams to butt up against each other for a perfect match. If you press the seam open, pin in the same way.

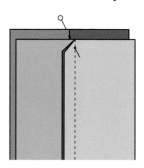

Place an extra pin on each side of the first pin with the points close to, but not over, the soon-to-be-stitched seam; remove the first pin.

BASTING SEAMS

Never sew over pins—you may break the needle, and the bulk of the pin, even a fine one, will cause wavy stitches. Instead, machine baste the pinned areas to ease any fullness and prevent shifting.

1. Baste the first pinned area with a long stitch, raise the needle and presser foot, and pull the fabric from under the presser foot.

2. Without breaking the threads, move to the next pinned area, lower the presser foot, and baste.

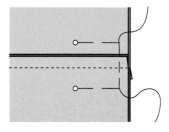

3. Baste the remaining pinned areas.

4. Remove the pins and check the basted areas for matched seams. If the seams don't match, rip out the basting and start again. Cut the threads.

5. Pin the rest of the fabric in place, easing in any fullness. Sew the entire seam using a regular stitch length. Carefully remove the basting.

SEWING SEAMS

When you sew over seams that are pressed to one side, sew with the top seam allowance pressed away from you and the bottom seam allowance pressed toward you. The presser foot will pull the top seam toward you enough to lock the seams together. As you sew, use the tip of a seam ripper to keep the top seam flat under the presser foot.

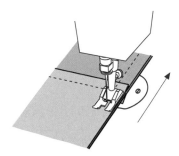

If you're sewing two pieces together and one is slightly shorter, place the longer piece on the bottom. The feed dogs will help ease the extra length or fullness as you stitch.

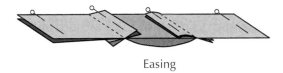

Easing

MATCHING BIAS SQUARES

To match bias squares, place the tip of the pin at the exact spot where the diagonal seams meet and ¼" from each raw edge. Always begin sewing at this intersecting corner to keep the diagonal seams in alignment.

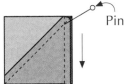

Pin

CHAIN PIECING

This assembly-line method is much faster than sewing one block at a time. My usual method is to sew one block first to get a feel for the pattern. Once I understand the steps, I chain-piece the rest of the blocks.

1. Place the pieces, as they are to be sewn, next to the sewing machine. Use a piece of folded scrap fabric, about 1" x 2", for starting and finishing seams. Begin by sewing across the piece of folded fabric.

Scrap

2. When you reach the edges, don't raise the presser foot. Rather, butt the raw edges of the pieces to be sewn against the edges of the scrap fabric and continue sewing. Feed the paired pieces or units under the presser foot in a continuous motion, with just a few connecting stitches.

3. After you finish the seam, don't raise the presser foot. Place another piece of folded scrap fabric at the end of your sewn pieces and sew across it for a few stitches. Leave the scrap fabric in place with the needle in the down position, ready for the next pieces.

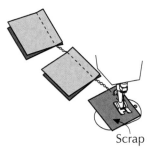

Scrap

4. When you're finished piecing, clip the few chain stitches between the scrap fabrics and the sewn pieces. Press all the units at one time.

STRIP PIECING

With this technique you sew strips together, then cut segments and assemble them to make blocks or units. In addition to being a great time saver, strip piecing is much more exact than cutting separate pieces and sewing them together.

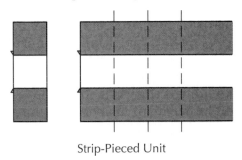

Strip-Pieced Unit

PRESERVING THE POINTS

It can't be said enough: accuracy is the key to making bias squares with near-perfect points. If your seam allowance is exactly ¼" wide and your piecing precise, the block seams will fall in just the right places, and you'll preserve the bias-square points. If your block measurements are off, you'll probably lose the points when you stitch the seams. On a miniature quilt, this error is very noticeable.

To maintain perfect points, check your sewing at every step, measuring your seams and pieces and correcting mistakes as you go.

Once you've completed a block, press it on both sides. With the block right side up, measure the finished dimensions, from future seam to future seam.

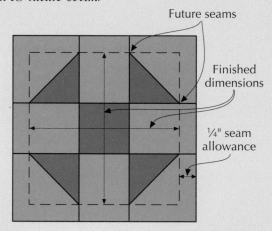

Future seams

Finished dimensions

¼" seam allowance

Or, make a template from ¼"-grid plastic template material, drawing the seam lines and the outer ¼"-wide seam allowances. Place the template on the right side of the block to see where you must make corrections.

If your block is off just a little, rip out and resew the seams until the block is accurate. If the block is way off, it's best to cut pieces for a new block. Starting over is faster than picking apart a crooked block and trying to sew edges that, by this time, may have stretched.

Any adjustments you make may result in a block with uneven edges or seam allowances that are less than a full ¼" wide. If that's the case, mark the seam lines on the wrong side of the block so the bias-square points are maintained.

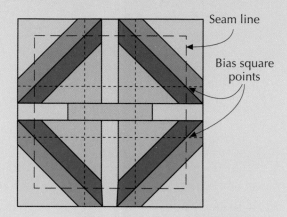

Seam line

Bias square points

Match the marked seam lines when you join blocks. If you mark the seam lines on your blocks, you'll also need to mark the seam lines on the wrong sides of triangles, sashing strips, and border strips that you join to the blocks. Match the marked seam lines when you pin and stitch the pieces.

When sewing over other points, such as the point of a diagonally set block, sew across the point exactly where the two seams meet and form an **X**. Place the side with the point on top so you can see this **X**.

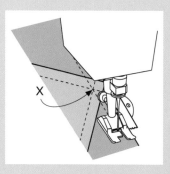

X

SEWING TRIANGLES

When joining triangles, trim the "rabbit ears" so the points will not interfere with the seaming.

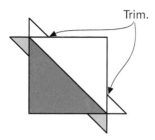

Trim.

When sewing a triangle to a block or a plain square, match the corner, with the square or block on top. Begin sewing from the right-angle corner.

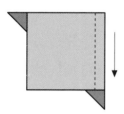

To sew a corner setting triangle to a diagonally set block, fold the triangle in half and crease it on the long edge. With right sides together and the triangle underneath, match the crease on the triangle to the midpoint of the block and pin. Pin the rest of the triangle to the block; stitch.

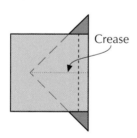

Crease

Pressing As You Sew

Pressing-as-you-sew is an essential technique in miniature quiltmaking. When you press after each seam, you see immediately whether or not you have sewn the pieces accurately. Correctly pressed seams are also necessary for precise piecing and seam matching.

Pressing involves gently touching the fabric with the tip of the iron. I generally prefer to press with a dry, hot iron; other miniature-quilt makers use steam. In either case, overpressing can distort the pieces, so use a light touch.

PRESSING POINTERS

Always use your iron to press; finger-pressing isn't adequate for miniature quilts.

The general rule of thumb is to press seams toward the darker fabric. If you press seams toward the lighter fabric, the darker seam allowances may show from the right side.

As you piece, you'll discover that seam allowances have a mind of their own and fall in the direction of least piecing. As you join smaller and smaller pieces, it becomes increasingly difficult to press seams toward the darker fabric. In this case, press the seams away from bulky areas regardless of the fabric color. With tiny pieces, I often press the seams open and trim them to ⅛" to reduce bulk.

PRESSING SEAMS FLAT

When you press opposing seams flat, to one side, it's easy to butt the seams against each other for an accurate, snug match.

1. To create a crisp, flat seam, lay the piece flat on the ironing board with the wrong side of the dark fabric facing up. Press the two pieces together to set the seam.
2. Using your free hand, lift the dark fabric and slip your iron under it. Gently push the dark fabric up and away from the seam. Press the seam flat with the tip of your iron.
3. Turn the piece to the wrong side and press again to make sure the seam allowance is pressed in the correct direction.

PRESSING SEAMS OPEN

It's easy to match seams that are pressed open, especially when the pieces are small.

1. Lay the piece wrong side up on the pressing surface. Use the index finger of your free hand to open the seam as you press it with the tip of the iron.
2. Turn the piece to the right side and press the seam again.

PRESSING ROW SEAMS

Press the blocks before joining them into rows. Once they're joined, press the seams in one direction on odd-numbered rows and the opposite direction on even-numbered rows.

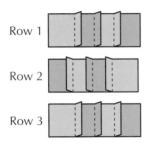

Setting Blocks

There are two classic ways to set quilt blocks: straight (with the blocks resting on one edge) or diagonally (with the blocks balanced "on point").

STRAIGHT SET

When you set blocks straight, side by side, it's easy to sew the blocks into rows, then join the rows. You can add sashing between blocks and rows in a straight setting. (See "Adding Sashing" at right.)

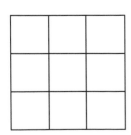
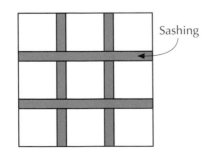

Straight Sets

You can also separate blocks with plain squares the same size as your pieced blocks. Plain squares have a number of advantages. They separate complicated blocks, reduce the number of pieced blocks needed for the quilt top, and provide plain areas to showcase quilting.

DIAGONAL SET

To avoid confusion when setting blocks diagonally, pin the blocks to a piece of flannel or foam-core board along with the plain squares, setting triangles, and sashing, if used. Join the pieces in diagonal rows.

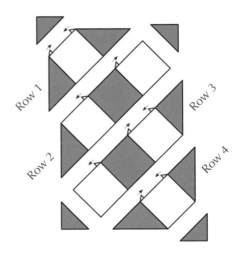

Join the diagonal rows, carefully matching block seams, then add the corner setting triangles.

Adding Sashing

Sashing, sometimes referred to as a lattice, consists of narrow strips of fabric used to separate individual blocks from each other or groups of blocks from the borders.

For the greatest stability, cut the sashing strips on the lengthwise grain. I cut my sashing strips no narrower than 1" wide. After seaming, the finished width is ½", wide enough to accommodate the two ¼"-wide seam allowances that butt against each other on the wrong side.

INNER SASHING

The short vertical strips that join blocks into rows and the longer horizontal strips that join rows are referred to as inner sashing strips.

TO ATTACH INNER SASHING STRIPS:

1. Press the blocks on both sides. Check and mark the seam lines, if necessary, on the blocks and sashing strips. (See "Preserving the Points" on page 22.)
2. With right sides together and raw edges aligned, pin a short sashing strip to the appropriate edge of the block. Position the block with the pressed seams toward you and the sashing strip on top.

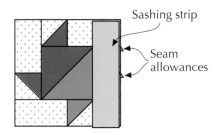

Sashing strip

Seam allowances

3. Stitch, using a ¼"-wide seam allowance and preserving the points. Press the seam toward the sashing.
4. To match the seams from block to block, lay the sewn piece flat with the wrong side up. Align your rotary ruler with the seams and mark the corresponding points on the opposite edge of the sashing.

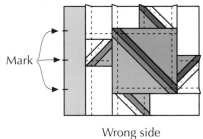

Mark

Wrong side

5. Sew the marked edge of the sashing to the next block, matching the block seams and marks.
6. Sew the remaining vertical sashing strips to the blocks. Press the seam allowances toward the sashing.

7. Sew the horizontal sashing strips to the rows, matching the vertical sashing seams. Press the seam allowances toward the sashing.

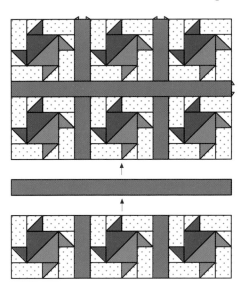

SEW-AND-TRIM METHOD

This technique ensures a uniform sashing width, which is useful for narrow sashing. Do not, however, use this method with directional prints, because the design may appear crooked when you trim the sashing.

1. Cut the sashing strip ¼" wider than needed. Sew the sashing strip to the block or row using a ¼"-wide seam allowance. Press the seam allowances toward the block and trim to ⅛".
2. Place the piece right side up and hold it firmly with your ruler to prevent shifting. Trim the sashing to the desired finished width plus ¼".

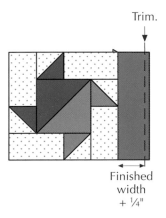

Trim.

Finished width + ¼"

3. Sew the remaining edge of the sashing strip to the block or row. Press both seam allowances toward the sashing. Trim to ⅛".

CORNERSTONES

Corner sashing squares, called cornerstones, add visual interest and introduce another color or print to a sashing structure.

1. Strip-piece the sashing and cornerstone fabrics. Make the unit 1" to 2" longer than necessary because, when the fabrics are pieced, the ends may be uneven. Press the seams away from the cornerstone strips so the seams will butt against the vertical sashing seams.

2. Join the horizontal sashing strips to the rows of blocks, using a ¼"-wide seam allowance and matching the vertical sashing seams. Press the seams toward the horizontal sashing.

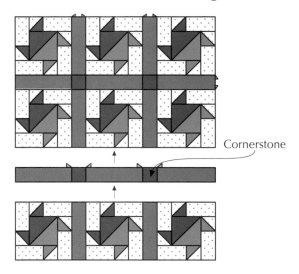

Cornerstone

OUTER SASHING

Outer sashing strips separate the blocks and inner sashing strips from the border.

Attach the outer sashing as you would a single straight border. (See the opposite page.) Be sure to maintain a full ¼"-wide seam allowance on each edge and preserve the points. (See page 22.)

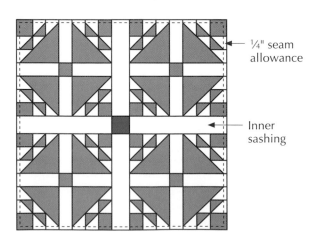

¼" seam allowance

Inner sashing

Squaring the Quilt Top

After the blocks are joined but before you attach the border strips, square the quilt top.

1. Lightly press the quilt top on both sides and check for proper seam pressing. I use a steam iron to make the quilt top lie flat.

2. Trim the quilt top, maintaining the ¼"-wide seam allowance and a 90° angle at each corner. If the raw edges are uneven, mark the seam allowance on the back of the quilt top, always preserving the points. (See page 22.)

On a straight-set quilt without sashing, there will probably be little, if anything, to trim. On a diagonally set quilt, you may need to trim the edges of the setting triangles. Be sure to maintain a 90° angle at each corner.

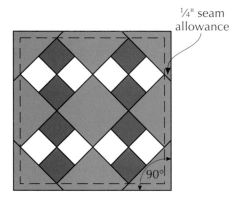

¼" seam allowance

90°

Adding Borders

To audition a border fabric, fold it into a piece that's larger than the quilt top. Lay the quilt top on the folded fabric, step back, and evaluate the effect. Does the border frame the quilt nicely from a distance? Are the fabrics in scale? Do the pieced area and border share common colors or designs? Repeat this auditioning process until you find the right fabric.

Typically, outer borders are the same finished width as the blocks, though the fabric's design may dictate wider borders. It's desirable to center any major motifs on the border strips.

For the greatest stability, cut the border strips on the lengthwise grain. If you wish to use the same fabric for the quilt blocks and borders, make sure you have enough before you cut.

STRAIGHT BORDERS

Straight borders may consist of single strips or multiple strips that meet at right angles at the corners. Straight borders are the easiest and fastest borders to sew.

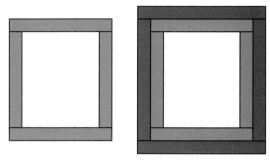

Straight Borders

Attaching Straight Borders

1. Measure the quilt top lengthwise through the center of the quilt. Trim the right and left border strips to this measurement. If you marked the seam lines on the backs of the blocks, also mark a seam line on the wrong side of each strip.

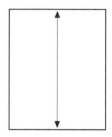

2. Fold each strip in half and crease to mark the midpoint. Measure and mark the midpoint on the right and left edges of the quilt top.

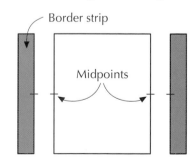

Border strip

Midpoints

3. With right sides together and the borders on top, pin the strips to the quilt top, matching the midpoints and the marked seam lines, if any. Pin the borders and quilt top at the ends. Finish pinning the strips to the quilt top, easing any fullness.

4. Stitch the borders to the quilt top. Use a ¼"-wide seam allowance or stitch along the marked seam lines. Press the seam allowances toward the borders.

5. For the upper and lower borders, measure the width of the quilt top through the center, including the right and left borders. Trim the border strips to this length.

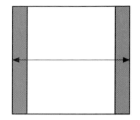

6. Pin and stitch the upper and lower strips to the quilt top as you did the right and left strips. Press the seam allowances toward the border.

BORDERS WITH CORNER SQUARES

"Maple Leaf" on page 35 and "Grecian" on page 39 feature borders with corner squares.

1. Measure the quilt top lengthwise and widthwise through the center. Trim the right and left border strips to the length measurement.
2. Follow steps 2–4 for "Straight Borders" to stitch the right and left border strips to the quilt top.
3. Trim the upper and lower border strips to the original width measurement of the quilt top. Sew the corner squares to the ends of these strips. Press the seam allowances toward the borders.
4. Pin and stitch the strips with corner squares to the upper and lower edges of the quilt, matching the seams at the corners.

MITERED BORDERS

Mitered borders add visual interest to a quilt, but they do require planning and careful sewing.

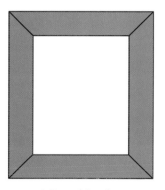

Mitered Border

Attaching Mitered Borders

1. Estimate the finished size of the quilt with the border. Add 3" to each measurement to arrive at the cut length of the strip. Cut the strips to the correct lengths. If you marked seam lines on the back of your blocks, also mark a seam line on the wrong side of each border strip.

2. Measure the pieced top through the center. Record the length and width, minus ½" each for seam allowances.

Length - ½" = _____

Width - ½" = _____

Width

Length

3. Fold each strip in half and crease to mark the midpoint. From this crease, measure and pin a distance equal to one-half the finished length or width measurement from step 2.

4. Measure and mark the midpoint on each edge of the quilt top. Also measure and mark the point ¼" from the edge at each corner.

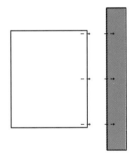

5. With right sides together and the borders on top, pin the strips to the quilt top, matching the midpoints, pins, and the marked seam lines, if any. Finish pinning the strips to the quilt top, easing any fullness.

6. Stitch, using a ¼"-wide seam allowance, or stitch along the marked seam lines. Begin and end the stitching ¼" from the edges; backstitch to secure. Press the seams toward the quilt.

7. Place the quilt right side up on the ironing board and fold the borders at 45° angles as shown. Press the folded corners and pin, one corner at a time.

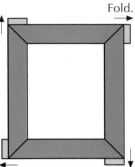

Fold.

8. Starting at one corner, remove the pins and fold the quilt on the diagonal, right sides together. Align the raw edges and border seams of the two strips. Pin the borders on either side of the fold.

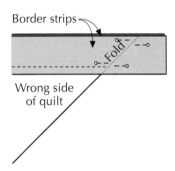

Border strips

Fold

Wrong side of quilt

9. Mark the fold. Stitch on the fold from the outside edge of the border toward the quilt top. Stop stitching at the border seam; backstitch to secure.

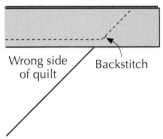

Wrong side of quilt

Backstitch

10. Stitch the remaining corners. Press the seams open. Turn the quilt right side up. Place your square ruler on each corner and align the 45° angle line with the mitered seam. If the corner isn't a 90° angle, rip out the stitches, press the border strips, and resew.

11. Press the seams closed and trim to ¼" wide; press the seams open again and trim the "rabbit ears." Press the seams joining the border to the quilt top toward the border strips.

Marking the Quilt Top

Mark the quilt top after you finish piecing but before you layer the top, batting, and backing. Test your markers on scraps of fabric used in the quilt to make sure the marks are easy to remove.

MARKING TOOLS

On light fabrics, I mark with a fine-point #2 mechanical pencil because the lead is soft and easy to erase. Use a light touch, or you may not be able to remove all the marks.

I also use a purple fading pen to mark light fabrics. Marks made by this pen disappear in twenty-four to seventy-two hours. Be aware that heat permanently sets the chemical, which means you can't iron your quilt top once it's been marked.

You may want to try colored pencils, available at quilt shops. A variety of light-colored pencils are useful for marking dark fabrics. Berol Verithin pencils in lemon yellow and silver are my favorites. Pencil-remover spray is available; be sure to follow the instructions carefully.

To create straight lines without marking the fabric, use ¼"-wide quilter's masking tape, available at quilt shops. Use a C-Thru ruler to position the tape.

I also use a small chalk wheel, available in several colors, with a rotary ruler. Brush or wipe off the chalk marks with a clean, damp cloth.

Layering the Quilt

Careful layering of your quilt top, batting, and backing ensures a smooth fabric "sandwich" for quilting.

BACKING FABRIC

Cut the backing fabric 1½" larger than the quilt top on all edges (3" larger than the length and width measurements) to allow for shrinkage and shifting during quilting. Spray the fabric with sizing and press it.

If your quilt is rectangular, cut the backing fabric on the lengthwise grain for a more stable fabric sandwich.

BATTING

I use two types of batting for most of my miniature quilts, low-loft polyester batting and cotton/polyester batting. On occasion, I use Thermore®, a very lightweight batting by Hobbs, because it's easy to quilt, doesn't shift, and gives a nice appearance. I don't use flannel as batting because it's too difficult to quilt.

Cut the batting 1" larger than the quilt top on all edges (2" larger than the length and width measurements) to allow for shrinkage and shifting during quilting.

Low-Loft Batting

Low-loft polyester batting is the puffiest when quilted. I use this batting when I want to achieve a contemporary look.

Because the surface is smooth, low-loft batting can cause the fabrics to shift, making it necessary to carefully baste the quilt top, batting, and backing. Low-loft batting quilts easily with a running stitch. (See page 30.)

Cotton/Polyester Batting

This batting, composed of 80% cotton and 20% polyester, gives a quilt a flatter appearance than polyester. I prefer to use cotton/polyester batting when I'm quilting vintage fabrics or when I want to create an old-fashioned look. To soften the piece of batting, wet it and dry it in the dryer with a fabric softener sheet.

If the batting is wrinkled, press it lightly with a steam iron. After I layer the quilt top, batting, and backing, I firmly press the "sandwich" on both sides with a steam iron set on "cotton."

Cotton/polyester batting is more difficult to quilt, and you must use the stab-and-jab stitch (see page 31), which takes longer than a running stitch. To achieve a slightly puffy effect, quilt parallel lines no farther apart than ½". (Parallel lines that are too far apart make the quilt look flat.)

THE QUILT TOP

Check the quilt top one last time for sewing inconsistencies, such as crooked seams or points that don't meet, and repair them if possible. If seam allowances have flipped to the wrong side, baste the seams into proper position before layering. Use a steam iron to press the quilt top on both sides.

PUTTING IT ALL TOGETHER

Lay your backing fabric on your work surface, wrong side up. Tape it down. Center the batting on the backing. Center the quilt top on the batting and backing.

Hand Basting

Pin the layers together with straight pins, easing any fullness. Baste across the length and width of the quilt top in parallel rows, then diagonally in both directions. Stay at least ¼" away from the seams and baste over the seams, not through them.

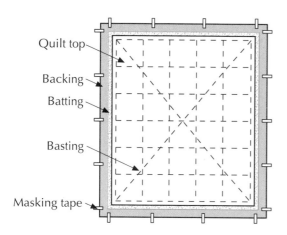

Quilt top
Backing
Batting
Basting
Masking tape

Pin Basting

I prefer to pin-baste my quilts with small brass safety pins, moving the pins as I quilt. Even though the quilting thread catches on the pins from time to time, the inconvenience is a small price to pay for not basting with thread.

Baste and quilt the interior portion of the quilt top before basting and quilting the borders.

Quilting the Quilt

I enjoy hand quilting immensely, and I think it's more appealing on miniatures than machine quilting. I've also discovered that I can quilt more complex designs by hand than by machine.

Fine hand quilting takes time and practice, and some quilters master it more quickly than others. The goal of hand quilting is small, evenly spaced stitches that show on both the quilt top and the back, with no knots or crossover stitches visible on the back. Initially, evenly spaced stitches are more important than small stitches. I prefer to do a minimum of quilting and add more if areas appear too plain. I object to over-quilting miniatures. Too much quilting "scrunches" the quilt, making it look wrinkled and distorted. With minimal quilting, the quilt retains its shape, and the piecing pattern and quilting design show clearly.

I suggest that you quilt with a hoop or frame; either will keep your quilt sandwich taut, making it easier to achieve small, evenly spaced stitches.

A thimble will protect your fingertip. In place of a thimble, you can use a rubber finger cap, available at office supply stores.

QUILTING STITCHES

Begin quilting by hiding the knot. Thread the needle and make a small knot at the end. Insert the needle in the top layer of a seam, about 1" from where you want to begin quilting. I usually start quilting at the center of the quilt, then work outward. Run the needle through the batting but do not pierce the backing fabric. Bring the needle up and gently pull the thread until you hear a pop, indicating that the knot is buried in the batting. Trim the tail.

The Running Stitch

Starting on the top of the quilt, with the needle parallel to the fabric, stitch up and down through the layers in a rocking motion, taking several stitches at a time. I find it easier to manipulate the fabric with my fingers rather than using the needle. Place your free hand under the quilt so you can feel when the needle has gone through the backing. As you work, turn the quilt over to check for consistent stitches.

Gently pull the thread through the fabric. If you pull the thread too tight, the fabric will bunch up. To end the line of quilting, make a small knot close to the last stitch. Run the needle through the batting only and bring it to the top at a seam; gently pull the thread until you hear a pop. Trim the tail.

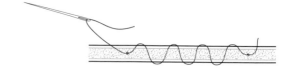

The Stab-and-Jab Stitch

This classic stitch is slower and more difficult to master for some quilters, but it does result in small, evenly spaced stitches. This stitch is appropriate for blocks that have many seams.

Place the needle point perpendicular to the quilt top and push it through to the back of the quilt. Gently pull the thread through the three layers.

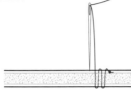

Place the needle point, perpendicular to the backing fabric, a short distance from the thread; push the needle to the top. Gently pull the thread to complete one stitch.

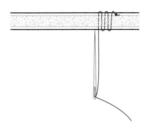

QUILTING DESIGNS

Stitching in-the-Ditch

If the pieces within each block are small, it's best to maintain the block design by quilting "in-the-ditch." This term refers to quilting so close to the seam that the stitches are barely noticeable. If you pressed the seam allowances to one side, quilt on the side without the seam allowance; the side with the seam allowance will look slightly raised.

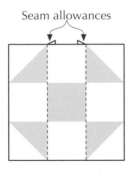

Seam allowances

Quilting "in-the-ditch"

On bias squares, I quilt in the middle of the seams to anchor the layers.

Outline Quilting

On blocks with larger pieces, you can outline quilt ⅛" or ¼" away from the seams. To quilt ⅛" from the seams, simply "eyeball" the distance. To quilt ¼" from seams, use quilter's masking tape.

Background Quilting

Background quilting is often used to fill in large, plain areas. Crosshatching is perhaps the most common form of background quilting. Use masking tape or measure and mark the quilting lines.

Motif Designs

Use motif designs, often referred to as block designs, in open areas, such as plain squares or borders. Motif designs should fill the intended area without crowding. Use a stencil to mark the design.

Outline Quilting   Background Quilting   Motif Design

Border Designs

Choose a compatible quilting design for the border. Avoid over-quilting the border—it detracts from the piecing and distorts the border fabric, making it difficult to achieve flat edges when you attach the binding.

Binding the Edges

Binding adds the finishing touch to your miniature quilt. I attach four separate binding strips to the edges of my quilts, but you may prefer another method.

Trim the edges of your quilt using your rotary cutter and ruler. Make sure each corner is a 90° angle.

It's best to cut binding strips for miniatures on the lengthwise grain, because lengthwise strips help keep the edges of the quilt flat.

1. Measure the length of the quilt through the center. Cut two strips, each 1" wide, equal to this measurement.
2. Fold each strip in half and crease to mark the midpoint. Measure and mark the midpoint on the right and left edges of the quilt top.
3. With right sides together and raw edges aligned, pin the right and left binding strips to the quilt top, matching the midpoints. Pin the ends, then ease any fullness between the pins.
4. Stitch the strips to the quilt top using a short stitch and a ¼"-wide seam allowance.

5. Lay the quilt on your work surface, wrong side up, and fold the binding to the back on each edge. Turn the binding under ¼" so that the raw edge just touches the raw edges of the quilt top.

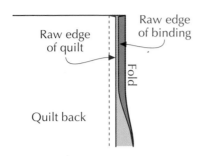

6. Fold the binding another ¼" so that it covers the seam allowance, and the first fold just touches the stitching. Pin at the midpoint, then at the ends. Pin the remainder of the binding strip, easing any fullness.

7. Blindstitch the binding to the back of the quilt; use matching thread and fine stitches. Make sure to catch only the fabric on the back of the quilt.

8. Measure the width of the quilt through the center, including the binding. Cut two strips, each 1" wide, equal to this measurement plus 2".

9. Pin the upper and lower binding strips as you did the side strips, with 1" extending beyond each edge. Trim the ends of the strips to ⅜" and fold them even with the edges of the quilt.

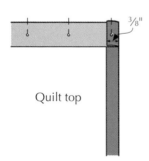

10. Stitch the upper and lower binding strips as you did the right and left strips. Fold the binding to the back of the quilt and blindstitch. Stitch each end closed and hide the knot.

SIGNING YOUR QUILT

It's important to document your quilt with your name, the name of the quilt, and the date completed. It's always nice to include interesting details, such as the origin of an unusual or vintage fabric or the source of the quilt pattern.

The simplest label consists of a piece of muslin. Stiffen the fabric by placing it against the shiny side of a piece of freezer paper and ironing. Write the information on the muslin, using a permanent-ink fabric pen, available at quilt shops. Peel away the freezer paper and sew the label to the back of your quilt at a lower corner.

Caring for Miniature Quilts

One of the simplest steps you can take to preserve your quilts is to wash your hands before handling them. Unseen dirt and oil soils quilts faster than you think.

Shake the dust out of your quilts from time to time. Avoid exposure to direct sunlight, which will fade and damage the fabric.

Further protect your quilts by using a stain-resistant spray. Do not saturate the quilt, and allow the fabric to dry between applications.

If you did not prewash your fabrics, it's best to dry-clean the quilt. Just remember to tell the cleaner not to press your quilt—or it will look like a pancake! Dry cleaning is also the best option for a quilt that has a spot or stain.

If you prewashed the fabrics, wash your quilt by placing it in a sink of cool water with Orvus paste or a capful of clear, sudsy ammonia. Soak the quilt until it's clean, then drain and rinse with cool water. Air dry the quilt flat on a towel. Never twist or wring a quilt.

Color Cues

*For a two-color scheme, select a variety of light, medium, and dark prints.
Including fabrics that don't match exactly adds vitality to a quilt design.*

*Overmatched fabrics blend in a miniature quilt, blurring the piecing design.
It's better to choose distinctly different fabrics.*

*Rich earth colors—beige, brown, gold, green, and black—combine naturally with red.
Unexpected pink and buttercup yellow lighten and brighten the scheme.*

Gallery

Fish School

By Christine Carlson, 1993, Norcross, Georgia, 12⅞" x 15". Tackle this original design when you're in the mood for a challenge. You'll have fun selecting small- and medium-scale fabrics in marine colors and nautical prints. The fish appear to float on a background of turquoise blue, thanks to oversized setting triangles.

Lawyer's Puzzle

By Christine Carlson, 1993, Norcross, Georgia, 14" x 14". Spirited colors and unusual prints mix it up in this bold quilt. Variety in the style and scale of the fabrics lends vitality to the design. The small Four Patch corner blocks visually balance the central area of the quilt.

Maple Leaf

By Christine Carlson, 1993, Norcross, Georgia, 10⅜" x 12½". Vibrant Maple Leaf blocks stand out against a soft backdrop of pink squares and setting triangles. Repeating two of the block prints in the pieced border and binding visually unifies the quilt.

Arrowhead

By Christine Carlson, 1993, Norcross, Georgia, 13½" x 13½". This quilt's graphic impact comes from setting four same-fabric "arrowheads" toward a matching center square. Narrow yellow sashing joins the blocks into quarter-sections; wider pink sashing frames the combined blocks. Vintage fabrics lend an authentic look.

Triangle Puzzle

By Christine Carlson, 1992, Clearwater, Florida, 16½" x 16½". A scrap lover's dream, this colorful quilt is surprisingly easy to assemble in straight rows. You can make a smaller version with twenty-four blocks and change the proportions of the border.

Jacob's Ladder

By Christine Carlson, 1993, Norcross, Georgia, 10" x 11½". Good color contrast is essential in a quilt pattern this small. If you look closely, you'll see that same-color blocks run diagonally across the quilt.

Sawtooth Flying Geese

By Christine Carlson, 1992, Clearwater, Florida, 17½" x 17½". An original setting and a classic red-white-and-blue color scheme combine for a striking quilt. Make it for the man in your life or as a Fourth of July celebration quilt.

Ninepatch Star

By Christine Carlson, 1993, Norcross, Georgia, 12¾" x 12¾". Setting the blocks on point creates rhythm and movement in this simple scrap quilt. The setting triangles frame the blocks, but you can add a border if you like.

Hourglass

By Christine Carlson, 1993, Norcross, Georgia, 12½" x 16". Almost any color combination works with this simple pattern. In the quilt shown here, two coordinating borders echo and repeat the block color scheme.

Tennessee

By Christine Carlson, 1993, Norcross, Georgia, 15¾" x 15¾". This handsome quilt features a mix of small-scale light and dark prints in twelve on-point blocks. For variety and visual interest, five of the blocks are rotated. Narrow black sashing creates a unit that floats on a backdrop of plaid setting triangles.

Grecian

By Christine Carlson, 1992, Clearwater, Florida, 10¾" x 13". Vintage fabrics from the author's collection make this miniature quilt a one-of-a-kind treasure. The light background fabric emphasizes the classic lines of the blocks; the reverse coloration would be equally effective. Pieced borders with corner squares frame the quilt.

Windmill

By Christine Carlson, 1993, Norcross, Georgia, 12½" x 16¼". Color is the tie that binds a medley of fabrics in this country quilt. Dark blocks, light sashing, and a plaid border create the illusion of depth. Rotating the straight-set blocks from row to row adds a soft sense of motion.

Bear Paw

By Christine Carlson, 1993, Norcross, Georgia, 14½" x 17½". Contrasting colors and a lively setting add a contemporary twist to a traditional quilt pattern. The stylized prints maintain the mood.

Pinwheel

By Christine Carlson, 1993, Norcross, Georgia, 8¼" x 10⅜". The bold geometric print used as the border inspired this quilt and suggested the block pattern and colors. The diagonal set accentuates the twirling pattern of the Pinwheel blocks; a striped binding adds the finishing touch.

Quilt Plans

This section contains step-by-step instructions and illustrations for making each of the fourteen quilts shown in the Gallery. Read the instructions for the quilt you're making before you begin.

The "Materials" section in each plan lists the fabrics you need. The fabric dimensions allow a few extra inches for miscuts and "breathing room" when you cut. As long as it provides enough fabric for cutting the required pieces, you can use a piece that's slightly larger or of a different shape.

To avoid running out of fabric when you cut, sketch your fabric to scale on ¼"-grid graph paper, then map out your cutting strategy, starting with the bias strips and borders.

The measurements in the quilt plans are "perfect measurements," meaning they are mathematically correct. In reality, it's difficult to replicate these perfect measurements in miniature quiltmaking. You may need to make adjustments when cutting sashing, border, and binding strips. Therefore, it's best to cut these pieces after you make your blocks.

Consult "Quiltmaking Basics" on pages 11–33 if you are unsure of any step in the process. Of particular importance are "Preserving the Points" on page 22 and "Squaring the Quilt Top" on page 26.

Finally, precision is the secret to success with miniature quilts. Take the time to cut and sew accurately and be willing to resew if necessary. You—and anyone lucky enough to receive one of your quilts—will be thrilled with the results.

Bear Paw

Making a miniature quilt with bias squares doesn't come any easier than this contemporary version of Bear Paw. Because the blocks are relatively large and the construction simple, it's an ideal project for beginning quilters.

❧

Finished Size: 14½" x 17½"

Finished Block Size: 3" x 3"

Color photo on page 40

Skill Level: Beginner

Techniques: Bias squares, a straight setting, and two straight borders

MATERIALS: 44"-WIDE FABRIC

½ yd. black print for blocks and border
½ yd. yellow print for blocks, border, and binding
17½" x 20½" piece of fabric for backing
16½" x 19½" piece of batting

CUTTING

All measurements include ¼"-wide seam allowances. Refer to "Cutting Bias Strips" on page 13.

From the black print, cut:
2 pieces, each 11" x 18". Stack the pieces, wrong sides up, and cut from each piece:
  3 bias strips, each 1¼" x 15½", for blocks.
  From the remainder, cut:
  12 squares, each 2" x 2", for blocks;
  2 strips, each 1¾" x 12½", for inner border;
  2 strips, each 1¾" x 12", for inner border.

From the yellow print, cut:
2 pieces, each 11" x 18". Stack the pieces, right sides up, and cut from each piece:
  3 bias strips, each 1¼" x 15½", for blocks.
  From the remainder, cut:
  12 squares, each 1¼" x 1¼", for blocks;
  12 rectangles, each 1¼" x 2¾", for blocks;
  12 rectangles, each 1¼" x 3½", for blocks;
  2 strips, each 1¾" x 15", for outer border;
  2 strips, each 1¾" x 14½", for outer border;
  2 strips, each 1" x 17½", for binding;
  2 strips, each 1" x 16½", for binding.

DIRECTIONS

Refer to "Quiltmaking Basics" on pages 11–33 for general instructions.

Piecing the Blocks

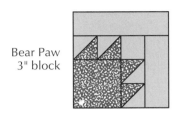

Bear Paw
3" block

Press the seam allowances in the direction of the small arrows or as instructed.

1. Sew a black bias strip to a yellow bias strip to make 1 bias set. Make a total of 6 bias sets. Press the seams open.

2. With the wrong sides of the bias sets facing up, cut 8 bias squares, each 1¼" x 1¼", from each set for a total of 48 bias squares. Trim the seams to ⅛".

3. Sew 2 bias squares together.

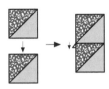

4. Sew the pair to the right edge of a 2" black square.

5. Sew 2 bias squares together. Sew a 1¼" yellow square to the right edge.

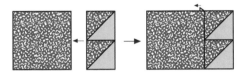

6. Sew the unit made in step 5 to the upper edge of the unit made in step 4, matching the seam.

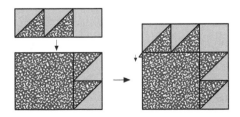

7. Sew a 1¼" x 2¾" yellow rectangle to the right edge of the unit made in step 6.

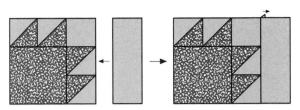

8. Sew a 1¼" x 3½" yellow rectangle to the upper edge of the unit made in step 7 to complete 1 Bear Paw block. Make a total of 12 blocks.

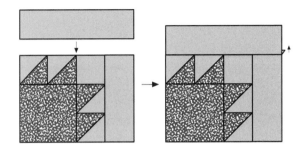

9. Press the blocks on both sides.

Assembling and Finishing the Quilt

1. Arrange the blocks in 4 horizontal rows of 3 blocks each as shown in the quilt plan. Join the blocks into rows. Press the seams in opposite directions from row to row.

2. Join the rows. Press the seams in the same direction.

3. Sew the 1¾" x 12½" black border strips to the right and left edges of the quilt top. Press the seams toward the border. Repeat with the 1¾" x 12" black border strips on the upper and lower edges.

4. Sew the 1¾" x 15" yellow border strips to the right and left edges of the quilt top. Press the seams toward the border. Repeat with 1¾" x 14½" yellow border strips on the upper and lower edges.

5. Press the quilt top on both sides and trim, if necessary.

6. Mark the top for quilting.

7. Layer the quilt top with batting and backing; baste. Quilt as desired.

8. Bind the edges with the 1"-wide yellow strips.

Lawyer's Puzzle

The use of color and design creates the illusion of complexity in this quilt, but you'll find the pattern surprisingly simple to make. The four large blocks are easily set with the sashing strips and Four Patch blocks.

❧

Finished Size: 14" x 14"

Finished Block Size: 3¾" x 3¾"

Color photo on page 34

Skill Level: Beyond Beginner

Techniques: Bias squares, quick-cut triangles, sashing, strip-pieced sashing, and Four Patch blocks

MATERIALS: 44"-WIDE FABRIC

½ fat quarter (11" x 18") of light turquoise print for blocks

½ fat quarter (11" x 18") of gold solid for blocks

5" x 9" piece of rose-and-black stripe for blocks

6" x 8" piece of black-and-white print for inner sashing

6" x 8" piece of pink print for inner sashing

8" x 12" piece of dark turquoise print for outer sashing

12" x 18" piece of purple print for outer sashing and binding

3" x 18" piece of bright fuchsia print for Four Patch blocks

3" x 18" piece of rose-and-blue polka dot print for Four Patch blocks

17" x 17" piece of fabric for backing

16" x 16" piece of batting

CUTTING

All measurements include ¼"-wide seam allowances. Refer to "Cutting Bias Strips" on page 13.

From the light turquoise print, wrong side up, cut:

4 bias strips, each 1¼" x 15½", for blocks.
   From the remainder, cut:
      2 squares, each 3⅞" x 3⅞", for blocks.

From the gold solid, right side up, cut:

4 bias strips, each 1¼" x 15½", for blocks.
   From the remainder, cut:
      4 squares, each 1¼" x 1¼", for blocks.

From the rose-and-black stripe, cut:

2 squares, each 3⅞" x 3⅞", for blocks.

From the black-and-white print, cut:

4 strips, each 1½" x 4¼", for inner sashing.

From the pink print, cut:

4 strips, each 1½" x 4¼", for inner sashing.

From the dark turquoise print, cut:
4 strips, each 1½" x 10", for outer sashing.

From the purple print, cut:
4 strips, each 1½" x 10", for outer sashing;
2 strips, each 1" x 14", for binding;
2 strips, each 1" x 16", for binding.

From the bright fuchsia print, cut:
1 strip, 1½" x 16", for Four Patch blocks.

From the rose-and-blue polka dot print, cut:
1 strip, 1½" x 16", for Four Patch blocks.

DIRECTIONS

*Refer to "Quiltmaking Basics" on pages
11–33 for general instructions.*

Piecing the Blocks

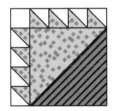

Lawyer's Puzzle
3¾" block

Press the seam allowances in the direction of the small arrows or as instructed.

1. Sew a gold bias strip to a light turquoise bias strip to make 1 bias set. Make a total of 4 bias sets. Press the seams open.
2. With the wrong sides of the bias sets facing up, cut 8 bias squares, each 1¼" x 1¼", from each set for a total of 32 bias squares. Trim the seams to ⅛".
3. Stack 2 light turquoise squares, each 3⅞", and cut in half once diagonally.
4. Sew 4 bias squares together. Sew this unit to the left edge of a triangle cut in step 3.

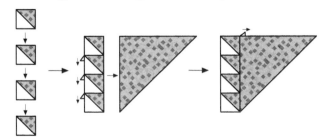

5. Sew 4 bias squares together. Sew a 1¼" gold square to the left edge. Sew this unit to the upper edge of the unit made in step 4, matching the seam.

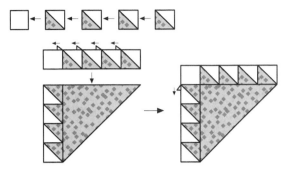

6. Stack the two rose-and-black stripe squares, each 3⅞", and cut in half once diagonally.
7. Sew the unit made in step 5 to a triangle cut in step 6 to complete 1 Lawyer's Puzzle block. Press the seam open and trim to ⅛". Make a total of 4 blocks.

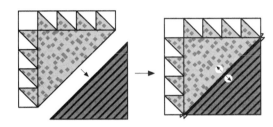

8. Press the blocks on both sides.
9. Sew a 1½" x 16" fuchsia strip to a 1½" x 16" rose-and-blue polka dot strip. Press the seam open. Cut 10 segments, each 1½" wide.

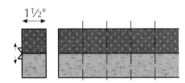

10. Sew 2 segments together, matching the center seam, to make 1 Four Patch block. Press the seam open. Make a total of 5 blocks.

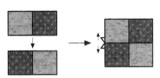

11. Press the blocks on both sides.
12. Sew 1 pink print inner sashing strip to 1 black-and-white inner sashing strip, each 1½" x 4¼", to make 1 inner sashing unit. Press the seam open. Make a total of 4 inner sashing units.
13. Sew 1 inner sashing unit vertically between a pair of Lawyer's Puzzle blocks. Repeat with the second pair. Press the seams toward the sashing.

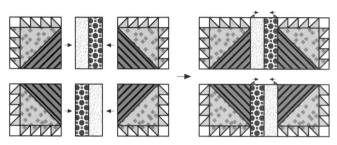

14. Sew 2 inner sashing units to 1 Four Patch block, matching the center seams. Press the seams toward the sashing.

15. Sew the pieced sashing unit horizontally between 2 pairs of blocks, matching the seams of the vertical sashing. Press the seams toward the sashing.

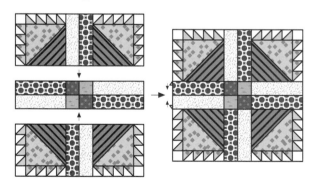

Assembling and Finishing the Quilt

1. Sew 1 dark turquoise outer sashing strip to 1 purple outer sashing strip, each 1½" x 10", to make 1 outer sashing unit. Press the seam open. Make a total of 4 outer sashing units.
2. Sew 2 outer sashing units to the right and left edges of the quilt top. Press the seams toward the sashing.
3. Sew a Four Patch block to each end of the remaining outer sashing units, matching the center seams, to make 2 pieced outer sashing units. Press the seams toward the sashing.

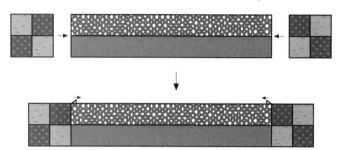

4. Sew the pieced outer sashing units to the upper and lower edges of the quilt top, matching the corner-square seams. Press the seams toward the sashing.
5. Press the quilt top on both sides and trim, if necessary.
6. Mark the top for quilting.
7. Layer the quilt top with batting and backing; baste. Quilt as desired.
8. Bind the edges with the 1"-wide purple strips.

Hourglass

It takes only five fabrics and six blocks to make this diagonally set quilt. Assembling the blocks is fast and easy because there are no bias squares that must be matched.

❧

Finished Size: 12½" x 16"

Finished Block Size: 2½" x 2½"

Color photo on page 38

Skill Level: Beginner

Techniques: Bias squares, quick-cut triangles, a diagonal setting, and two straight borders

MATERIALS: 44"-WIDE FABRIC

9" x 15" piece of beige muslin for blocks
½ fat quarter (11" x 18") of gold print for blocks
14" x 15" piece of multicolored floral print for blocks and inner border
11½" x 12½" piece of medium blue print for plain squares and setting triangles
13" x 18" piece of dark red print for outer border and binding
15½" x 19" piece of fabric for backing
14½" x 18" piece of batting

CUTTING

All measurements include ¼"-wide seam allowances. Refer to "Cutting Bias Strips" on page 13.

From the beige muslin, wrong side up, cut:
2 bias strips, each 1⅜" x 12½", for blocks.

From the gold print, cut:
1 piece, 9" x 15", for blocks. With the right side up, cut:
    2 bias strips, each 1⅜" x 12½", for blocks.
    From the remainder, cut:
    12 squares, each 1⅜" x 1⅜", for blocks.

From the floral print, cut:
6 squares, each 3" x 3", for blocks;
2 strips, each 1¾" x 11", for inner border;
2 strips, each 1¾" x 10", for inner border.

From the blue print, cut:
2 squares, each 3" x 3", for plain squares;
2 squares, each 4¾" x 4¾", for side setting triangles;
2 squares, each 2⅝" x 2⅝", for corner setting triangles.

From the red print, cut:
2 strips, each 1¾" x 13½", for outer border;
2 strips, each 1¾" x 12½", for outer border;
2 strips, each 1" x 16", for binding;
2 strips, each 1" x 14½", for binding.

DIRECTIONS

*Refer to "Quiltmaking Basics" on pages
11–33 for general instructions.*

Piecing the Blocks

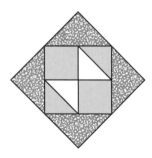

Hourglass
2½" block

Press the seam allowances in the direction of the small arrows or as instructed.

1. Sew a muslin bias strip to a gold bias strip to make 1 bias set. Make an additional bias set. Press the seams open.

2. With the wrong sides of the bias sets facing up, cut 6 bias squares, each 1⅜" x 1⅜", from each set for a total of 12 bias squares. Trim the seams to ⅛".

3. Sew a 1⅜" gold square to a bias square. Make 2 pairs.

4. Sew 2 pairs together, matching the center seam, to make 1 unit.

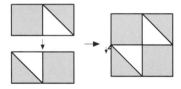

5. Stack 6 floral print squares, each 3", and cut in half twice diagonally.

6. Sew 4 floral print triangles cut in step 5 to the edges of the unit made in step 4 to complete 1 Hourglass block. Press the seams toward the triangles. Make a total of 6 blocks.

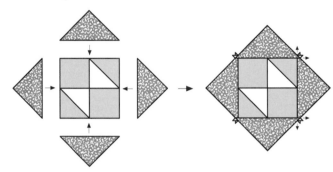

7. Press the blocks on both sides.

8. Stack 2 blue squares, each 4¾", and cut in half twice diagonally for the side setting triangles. Set aside 2 triangles.

Assembling and Finishing the Quilt

1. Arrange the 6 pieced blocks, two 3" blue squares, and 6 side setting triangles into 4 diagonal rows. Join the blocks into rows. Press the seams toward the plain squares and setting triangles.

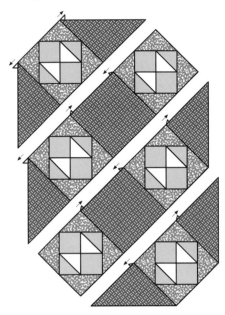

2. Join the rows. Press the seams open or in the same direction.
3. Stack 2 blue squares, each 2⅝", and cut in half once diagonally for the corner setting triangles.

4. Sew the triangles cut in step 3 to the quilt-top corners. Press the seams toward the triangles.

5. Sew the 1¾" x 11" floral border strips to the right and left edges of the quilt top. Press the seams toward the border. Repeat with the 1¾" x 10" floral strips on the upper and lower edges.
6. Sew the 1¾" x 13½" red border strips to the right and left edges of the quilt top. Press the seams toward the border. Repeat with the 1¾" x 12½" border strips on the upper and lower edges.
7. Press the quilt top on both sides and trim, if necessary.
8. Mark the top for quilting.
9. Layer the quilt top with batting and backing; baste. Quilt as desired.
10. Bind the edges with the 1"-wide red print strips.

Windmill

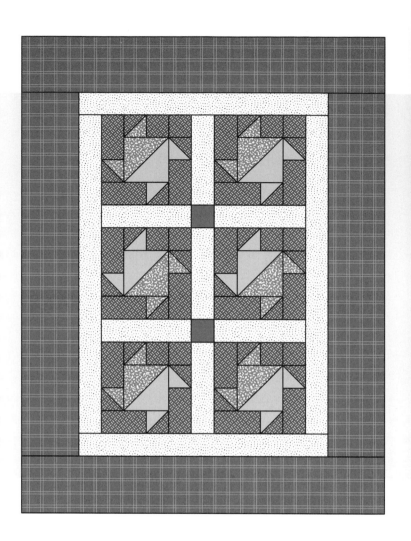

A 3" block and a minimum of pieces make this miniature quilt an ideal advanced-beginner project. You cut the sashing strips and cornerstones from a strip-pieced unit.

Finished Size: 12½" x 16¼"

Finished Block Size: 3"

Color photo on page 39

Skill Level: Beyond Beginner

Techniques: Bias squares, quick-cut triangles, sashing, strip-pieced sashing, and one straight border

MATERIALS: 44"-WIDE FABRIC

11" x 22" piece of dark green print for blocks
15" x 18" piece of dark gold print for blocks and binding
9" x 14" piece of brick red print for blocks
11" x 13" piece of beige print for sashing
3" x 4" piece of dark red print for cornerstones
11" x 14" piece of plaid for border
15½" x 19¼" piece of fabric for backing
14½" x 18¼" piece of batting

CUTTING

All measurements include ¼"-wide seam allowances. Refer to "Cutting Bias Strips" on page 13.

From the dark green print, cut:
1 piece, 9" x 18", for blocks. With the wrong side up, cut:
   4 bias strips, each 1¼" x 12½", for blocks.

From the remainder, cut:
   12 squares, each 1¼" x 1¼", for blocks;
   18 rectangles, each 1¼" x 2", for blocks.

From the dark gold print, cut:
1 piece, 9" x 14", for blocks. With the right side up, cut:
   2 bias strips, each 1¼" x 12½", for blocks.
From the remainder, cut:
   3 squares, each 2⅜" x 2⅜", for blocks;
   2 strips, each 1" x 16¼", for binding;
   2 strips, each 1" x 14½", for binding.

From the brick red print, right side up, cut:
2 bias strips, each 1¼" x 12½", for blocks.
   From the remainder, cut:
   3 squares, each 2⅜" x 2⅜", for blocks.

From the beige print, cut:
3 strips, each 1¼" x 3½", for sashing;
2 squares, each 3½" x 3½", for sashing;
2 strips, each 1¼" x 11", for sashing;
2 strips, each 1¼" x 8¾", for sashing.

From the dark red print, cut:
1 strip, 1¼" x 3½", for cornerstones.

From the plaid, cut:
2 strips, each 2⅜" x 12½", for border;
2 strips, each 2⅜" x 12½", for border.

DIRECTIONS

*Refer to "Quiltmaking Basics" on pages
11–33 for general instructions.*

Piecing the Blocks

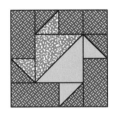

Windmill
3" block

Press the seam allowances in the direction of the
small arrows or as instructed.

1. Sew a green bias strip to a gold bias strip to make
   1 bias set. Make an additional bias set. Press the
   seams open.
2. With the wrong sides of the bias sets facing up,
   cut 6 bias squares, each 1¼" x 1¼", from each
   set for a total of 12 bias squares. Trim the seams
   to ⅛".
3. Repeat with 2 green bias strips and 2 brick red
   bias strips.
4. Stack 3 gold and 3 brick red squares, each 2⅜",
   and cut in half once diagonally.
5. Sew 1 gold and 1 brick red triangle cut in step 4
   together to make 1 seamed square. Press the
   seam open and trim to ⅛". Make a total of 6
   squares.

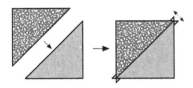

6. Press the squares on both sides and trim to 2",
   if necessary.
7. Sew a brick-red-and-green bias square to a 1¼"
   green square. Sew this unit to the upper edge of
   a gold-and-brick-red seamed square made in
   step 5.

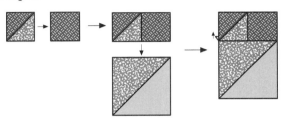

8. Sew a brick-red-and-green bias square to a
   1¼" x 2" green rectangle. Sew this unit to the
   left edge of the unit made in step 7.

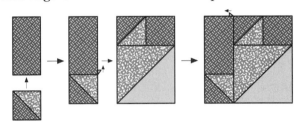

9. Sew a green-and-gold bias square to a 1¼" x 2"
   green rectangle. Sew this unit to the lower edge
   of the unit made in step 8.

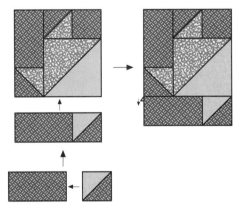

10. Sew a green-and-gold bias square to a 1¼" green square. Sew this unit to a 1¼" x 2" green rectangle.

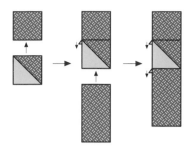

11. Sew the unit made in step 10 to the right edge of the unit made in step 9, matching the seam, to complete 1 Windmill block. Make a total of 6 blocks.

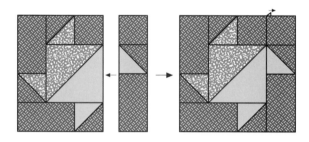

12. Press the blocks on both sides.

Assembling and Finishing the Quilt

1. Arrange the blocks in 3 pairs as shown in the quilt plan. Sew a 1¼" x 3½" beige sashing strip between each pair. Press the seams toward the sashing.

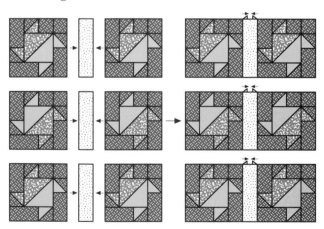

2. Sew the 1¼" x 3½" dark red rectangle between two 3½" beige squares to make 1 strip unit. Press the seams toward the sashing. Cut into 2 segments, each 1¼" wide.

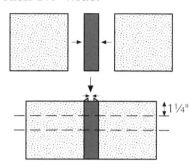

3. Sew the sashing units made in step 2 horizontally between the 3 rows of blocks, matching the vertical sashing seams. Press the seams toward the sashing.

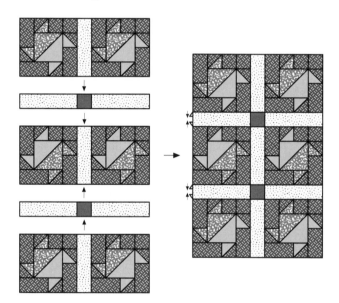

4. Sew the 1¼" x 11" beige sashing strips to the right and left edges of the quilt top. Press the seams toward the sashing. Repeat on the upper and lower edges with the 1¼" x 8¾" beige strips.

5. Sew the 2⅜" x 12½" plaid border strips to the right and left edges of the quilt top. Press the seams toward the border. Repeat with the 2⅜" x 12½" plaid strips on the upper and lower edges.

6. Press the quilt top on both sides and trim, if necessary.

7. Mark the top for quilting.

8. Layer the quilt top with batting and backing; baste. Quilt as desired.

9. Bind the edges with the 1"-wide gold strips.

Arrowhead

If you've never made a quilt with both inner and outer sashing, this project shows you how it's done. The four matching blocks in each quarter-section are easy to assemble. You cut the sashing, with cornerstones, from strip-pieced units.

❧

Finished Size: 13½" x 13½"

Finished Block Size: 2¼" x 2¼"

Color photo on page 35

Skill Level: Advanced Beginner

Techniques: Bias squares, sashing, strip-pieced sashing, and a straight setting

MATERIALS: 44"-WIDE FABRIC

½ fat quarter (11" x 18") each of 4 assorted prints for blocks

1 fat quarter (18" x 22") of yellow solid for blocks and inner sashing

7" x 20" piece of pink solid for outer sashing

6½" x 7" piece of brown print for cornerstones

16½" x 16½" piece of fabric for backing

6" x 17" piece of green solid for binding

15½" x 15½" piece of batting

CUTTING

All measurements include ¼"-wide seam allowances. Refer to "Cutting Bias Strips" on page 13.

From the 4 assorted prints, stacked wrong sides up, cut from each piece:
2 bias strips, each 1¼" x 15½", for blocks;
5 squares, each 1¼" x 1¼", for blocks;
4 squares, each 2" x 2", for blocks.

From the yellow solid, cut:
2 pieces, each 11" x 18". Stack the pieces, right sides up, and cut from each piece:
  3 bias strips, each 1¼" x 15½", for blocks.
  From each of 2 remaining triangles, cut:
  1 bias strip, 1¼" x 15½", for blocks.
  From the remainder, cut:
  16 strips, each 1¼" x 2¾", for inner sashing.

From the pink solid, cut:
6 strips, each 1½" x 5¾", for outer sashing;
2 strips, each 5½" x 5¾", for outer sashing.

From the brown print, cut;
3 strips, each 1½" x 5½", for cornerstones.

From the green solid, cut:
2 strips, each 1" x 13½", for binding;
2 strips, each 1" x 15½", for binding.

DIRECTIONS

Refer to "Quiltmaking Basics" on pages 11–33 for general instructions.

Piecing the Blocks

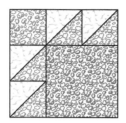

Arrowhead
2¼" block

Press the seam allowances in the direction of the small arrows or as instructed.

1. Sew a yellow bias strip to a print bias strip to make 1 bias set. Make an additional bias set. Press the seams open.

2. With the wrong sides of the bias sets facing up, cut 8 bias squares, each 1¼" x 1¼", from each set for a total of 16 bias squares. Trim the seams to ⅛".

3. Sew 2 bias squares together. Sew the pair to the left edge of a matching 2" print square.

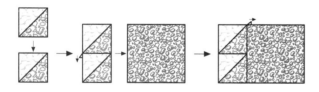

4. Sew 2 bias squares together. Sew a matching 1¼" print square to the left edge.

5. Sew the unit made in step 4 to the upper edge of the unit made in step 3, matching the seam, to complete 1 Arrowhead block. Make a total of 4 matching blocks.

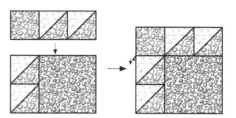

6. Press the blocks on both sides.

7. Arrange the 4 blocks so that each points inward. Sew a 1¼" x 2¾" yellow sashing strip vertically between each pair of blocks. Press the seams toward the sashing.

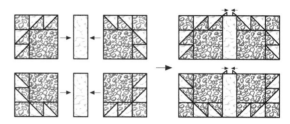

8. Sew a 1¼" matching square between two 1¼" x 2¾" yellow sashing strips to make a pieced sashing strip. Press the seams toward the sashing.

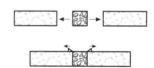

9. Sew the pieced sashing strip horizontally between the 2 rows of blocks, matching the vertical seams, to complete 1 quarter-section. Press the seams toward the sashing. Using the remaining prints and yellow solid, make a total of 4 quarter-sections.

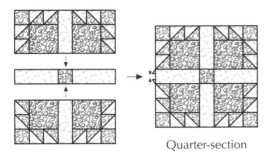

Quarter-section

Assembling and Finishing the Quilt

1. Arrange the 4 quarter-sections as shown in the quilt plan. Sew a 1½" x 5¾" pink sashing strip vertically between 2 quarter-sections and to the right and left edges of the quarter-sections. Press the seams toward the sashing.

Quarter-section

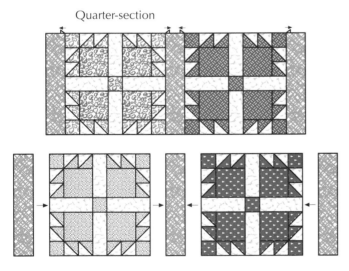

2. Sew the 5½" x 5¾" pink pieces between the 1½" x 5½" brown pieces to make a strip unit. Press the seams toward the pink pieces. Cut the unit into 3 sashing strips, each 1½" wide.

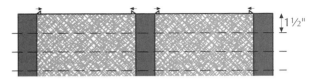

3. Sew a 1½"-wide pink-and-brown sashing strip cut in step 2 horizontally between the 2 rows and to the upper and lower edges, matching the vertical sashing seams. Press the seams toward the sashing.

4. Press the quilt top on both sides and trim, if necessary.

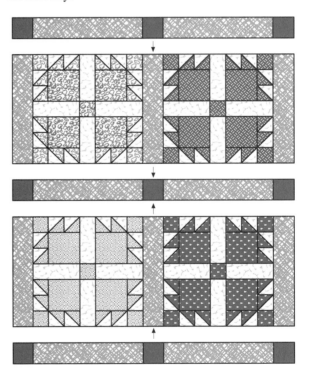

5. Mark the top for quilting.
6. Layer the quilt top with batting and backing; baste. Quilt as desired.
7. Bind the edges with the 1"-wide green strips.

Pinwheel

Each Pinwheel block consists of four bias squares. With careful piecing and pressing, you'll find it easy to match the bias-square points at the center of each block.

~

Finished Size: 8¼" x 10⅜"

Finished Block Size: 1½" x 1½"

Color photo on page 40

Skill Level: Beyond Beginner

Techniques: Bias squares, quick-cut triangles, a diagonal setting, and one mitered border

MATERIALS: 44"-WIDE FABRIC

6" x 9" piece each of 5 assorted solids for blocks
14" x 18" piece of white for blocks
11" x 15" piece of print for borders
11¼" x 13⅜" piece of fabric for backing
6" x 14" piece of black-and-white stripe for binding
10¼" x 12⅜" piece of batting

CUTTING

All measurements include ¼"-wide seam allowances. Refer to "Cutting Bias Strips" on page 13.

From the 5 assorted solids, stacked wrong sides up, cut:
1 bias strip, 1¼" x 8½", for blocks.
   From a leftover triangle, cut:
      1 bias strip, 1¼" x 8½", for blocks.

From the white, cut:
3 pieces, each 6" x 9", for blocks and setting triangles. Stack the pieces, right sides up, and cut from each piece:
   2 bias strips, each 1¼" x 8½", for blocks.
   From the remainder, cut:
   2 squares, each 2" x 2", for plain squares;
   2 squares, each 3⅜" x 3⅜", for side setting triangles;
   2 squares, each 2" x 2", for corner setting triangles.

From the print, cut:
2 strips, each 2¼" x 10¼", for borders;
2 strips, each 2¼" x 12⅜", for borders.

From the black-and-white stripe, cut:
2 strips, each 1" x 10⅜", for binding;
2 strips, each 1" x 10¼", for binding.

DIRECTIONS

*Refer to "Quiltmaking Basics" on pages
11–33 for general instructions.*

Piecing the Blocks

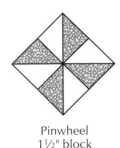

Pinwheel
1½" block

Press the seams in the direction of the small
arrows or as instructed.

1. Sew a white bias strip to a solid bias strip to make
   1 bias set. Make a total of 6 bias sets. Press the
   seams open.
2. With the wrong sides of the bias sets facing up,
   cut 4 bias squares, each 1¼" x 1¼", from each
   set for a total of 24 bias squares. Trim the seams
   to ⅛".
3. Sew 2 matching bias squares together to make
   1 unit. Make a second matching unit. Press the
   seams open and trim to ⅛".

4. Sew 2 units together, matching the center seam,
   to make 1 Pinwheel block. Press the seam open
   and trim to ⅛". Make a total of 6 blocks.

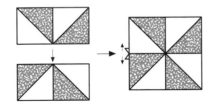

5. Press the blocks on both sides.
6. Stack 2 white squares, each 3⅜", and cut in half
   twice diagonally for the side setting triangles.
   Set aside 2 triangles.

Assembling and Finishing the Quilt

1. Arrange the 6 pieced blocks, two 2" white
   squares, and 6 side setting triangles into 4
   diagonal rows. Join the blocks into rows. Press
   the seams toward the plain squares and setting
   triangles.

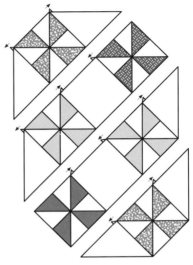

2. Join the rows. Press the seams open or in the
   same direction.
3. Stack 2 white squares, each 2", and cut in half
   once diagonally for the corner setting triangles.
4. Sew the triangles cut in step 3 to the quilt-top
   corners. Press the seams toward the triangles.

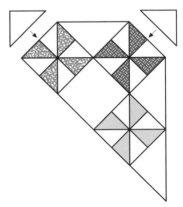

5. Referring to "Mitered Borders" on pages 27–28,
   sew the 2¼" x 12⅜" print strips to the right and
   left edges of the quilt top. Repeat with the
   2¼" x 10¼" print strips on the upper and lower
   edges.
6. Press the quilt top on both sides and trim, if
   necessary.
7. Mark the top for quilting.
8. Layer the quilt top with batting and backing;
   baste. Quilt as desired.
9. Bind the edges with the 1"-wide black-and-
   white stripe strips.

Triangle Puzzle

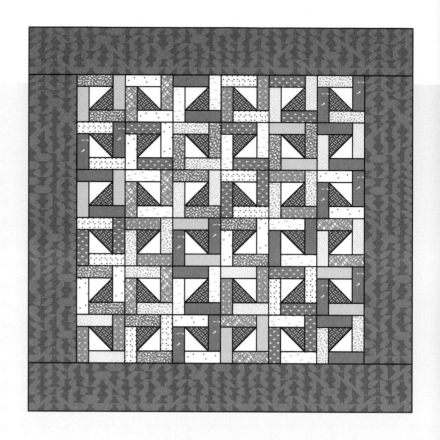

Although this scrap quilt looks complicated, it's one of the easiest patterns to make. Each block is composed of one bias square surrounded by two light strips and two dark strips.

Finished Size: 16½" x 16½"

Finished Block Size: 2" x 2"

Skill Level: Beginner

Color photo on page 36

Techniques: Bias squares, a straight setting, and one straight border

MATERIALS: 44"-WIDE FABRIC

11" x 14" piece each of 6 assorted dark blue prints for blocks
18" x 22" piece of beige muslin for blocks
1 fat quarter (18" x 22") of medium blue print for border and binding
36 assorted light print squares, each 3" x 3", for blocks
36 assorted dark print squares, each 3" x 3", for blocks
19½" x 19½" piece of fabric for backing
18½" x 18½" piece of batting

CUTTING

All measurements include ¼"-wide seam allowances. Refer to "Cutting Bias Strips" on page 13.

From the 6 assorted dark blue prints, stacked wrong sides up, cut from each piece:
1 bias strip, 1½" x 15½", for blocks.

From the beige muslin, cut:
2 pieces, 11" x 18". Stack the pieces, right sides up, and cut from each piece:
   3 bias strips, each 1½" x 15½", for blocks.

From the medium blue print, cut:
2 strips, each 2½" x 12½", for border;
2 strips, each 2½" x 16½", for border;
2 strips, each 1" x 16½", for binding;
2 strips, each 1" x 18½", for binding.

DIRECTIONS

Refer to "Quiltmaking Basics" on pages 11–33 for general instructions.

Piecing the Blocks

Triangle Puzzle
2" block

Press the seam allowances in the direction of the small arrows or as instructed.

1. Sew a muslin bias strip to a dark blue bias strip to make 1 bias set. Make a total of 6 bias sets. Press the seams open.

2. With the wrong sides of the bias sets facing up, cut 6 bias squares, each 1½" x 1½", from each set for a total of 36 bias squares. Trim the seams to ⅛".

3. Distribute the bias squares randomly in 9 groups of 4 bias squares each.

4. Stack the light and dark 3" squares and cut in half to make 72 light and 72 dark strips, each 1" x 2".

5. Sew a dark strip to the upper edge of a bias square, beginning at the right edge and sewing approximately 1". Flip the strip right side up and press.

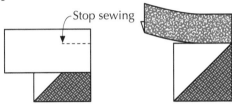

6. Sew a light strip to the right edge of the unit.

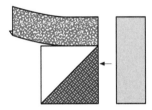

7. Sew a matching dark strip to the lower edge of the unit.

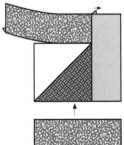

8. Fold and pin the free end of the first strip out of the way. Sew a matching light strip to the left edge of the unit.

9. Finish sewing the first strip to the upper edge of the unit to complete 1 Triangle Puzzle block. Make a total of 36 scrap blocks.

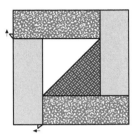

10. Press the blocks on both sides.

Assembling and Finishing the Quilt

1. Sew 4 blocks together, matching the block seams, to make 1 block unit. Make a total of 9 block units.

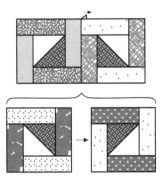

2. Arrange the block units in 3 horizontal rows of 3 units each, as shown in the quilt plan. Join the block units into rows, matching the block seams. Press the seams in opposite directions.

3. Join the rows, matching the block seams. Press the seams in the same direction.

4. Sew the 2½" x 12½" medium blue strips to the right and left edges of the quilt top. Press the seams toward the border. Repeat with the 2½" x 16½" medium blue strips on the upper and lower edges.

5. Press the quilt top on both sides and trim, if necessary.

6. Mark the top for quilting.

7. Layer the quilt top with batting and backing; baste. Quilt as desired.

8. Bind the edges with the 1"-wide medium blue print strips.

Grecian

Although the blocks in this quilt are easy to assemble, match the seams carefully when setting the blocks side-by-side. You sew the corner squares to strip-pieced border units.

❧

Finished Size: 10¾" x 13"

Finished Block Size: 2¼" x 2¼"

Color photo on page 39

Skill Level: Beyond Beginner

Techniques: Bias squares, strip piecing, a straight setting, and two straight borders with corner squares

MATERIALS: 44"-WIDE FABRIC

1 fat quarter (18" x 22") of light print for blocks
6" x 9½" piece each of 12 assorted medium prints for blocks
7" x 11½" piece of green print for inner border
8" x 11½" piece of red print for outer border
6" x 6" piece of light floral print for corner squares
13¾" x 16" piece of fabric for backing
5" x 15" piece of gold print for binding
12¾" x 15" piece of batting

CUTTING

All measurements include ¼"-wide seam allowances. Refer to "Cutting Bias Strips" on page 13.

From the light print, cut:
3 pieces, each 6" x 12". Stack the fabrics, wrong sides up, and cut from each piece:
    2 bias strips, each 1¼" x 8½", for blocks.
    From each of the 6 leftover triangles, cut:
        1 bias strip, 1¼" x 8½", for blocks.

From the remainder, cut:
12 pieces, each ⅞" x 6½", for blocks;
12 squares, each 1¼" x 1¼", for blocks.

From the 12 assorted medium prints, stacked right sides up, cut from each piece:
1 bias strip, 1¼" x 8½", for blocks.
    From the remainder, cut:
    1 strip, ⅞" x 6½", for blocks.

From the green print, cut:
2 strips, each 1¼" x 9½", for inner border;
2 strips, each 1¼" x 7¼", for inner border.

From the red print, cut:
2 strips, each 1½" x 9½", for outer border;
2 strips, each 1½" x 7¼", for outer border.

From the light floral print, cut:
4 squares, each 2¼" x 2¼", for corner squares.

From the gold print, cut:
2 strips, each 1" x 13", for binding;
2 strips, each 1" x 12¾", for binding.

DIRECTIONS

Refer to "Quiltmaking Basics" on pages 11–33 for general instructions.

Piecing the Blocks

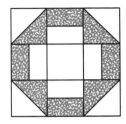

Grecian
2¼" block

Press the seam allowances in the direction of the small arrows or as instructed.

1. Sew 1 light bias strip to 1 medium bias strip to make 1 bias set. Press the seam open.
2. With the wrong side of the bias set facing up, cut 4 bias squares, each 1¼". Trim the seams to ⅛".
3. Sew a ⅞" x 6½" light strip to a matching ⅞" x 6½" medium strip to make 1 strip unit. Press the seam open and trim to ⅛". Cut 4 segments, each 1¼" wide.

4. Sew a bias square to opposite edges of a segment cut in step 3. Make an additional unit. Press the seams open and trim to ⅛".

5. Sew a 1¼" segment cut in step 3 to opposite edges of a 1¼" light print square to make 1 unit. Press the seams open and trim to ⅛".

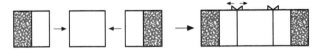

6. Sew the units made in step 4 to the unit made in step 5, matching the seams, to complete 1 Grecian block. Press the seams open and trim to

⅛". Using the remaining assorted print fabrics, make a total of 12 scrap blocks.

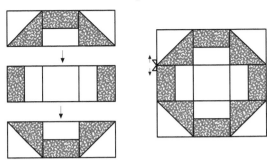

7. Press the blocks on both sides.

Assembling and Finishing the Quilt

1. Arrange the blocks in 4 horizontal rows of 3 blocks each as shown in the quilt plan. Join the blocks into rows, matching the seams. Press the seams in opposite directions.
2. Join the rows. Press the seams open.
3. Sew a 1¼" x 9½" green border strip to a 1½" x 9½" red border strip to make 1 border unit. Press the seam toward the red strip. Make an additional border unit. Sew the border units to the right and left edges of the quilt top. Press the seams toward the border.
4. Sew a 1¼" x 7¼" green border strip to a 1½" x 7¼" red border strip to make 1 border unit. Press the seam toward the red strip. Make an additional border unit. Sew a 2¼" floral square to each end of the border units to make 2 pieced borders. Press the seams toward the border.

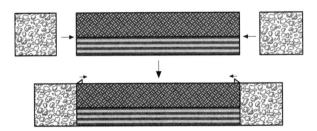

5. Sew the pieced borders to the upper and lower edges of the quilt top, matching the corner-square seams. Press the seams toward the border.
6. Press the quilt top on both sides and trim, if necessary.
7. Mark the top for quilting.
8. Layer the quilt top with batting and backing; baste. Quilt as desired.
9. Bind the edges with the 1"-wide gold strips.

Ninepatch Star

As the name implies, Ninepatch and Star blocks combine in this easy-to-make scrap quilt. You need to match only two seams when setting blocks diagonally.

❧

Finished Size: 12¾" x 12¾"

Finished Block Size: 3" x 3"

Color photo on page 37

Skill Level: Beyond Beginner

Techniques: Bias squares, strip piecing, quick-cut triangles, and a diagonal setting

MATERIALS: 44"-WIDE FABRIC

9½" x 14" piece of red print for Ninepatch blocks and corner setting triangles

3" x 14" piece of yellow print #1 for Ninepatch blocks

5" x 8" piece of yellow print #2 for Ninepatch blocks

½ fat quarter (11" x 18") each of 3 assorted dark blue prints for Star blocks

½ yd. of beige muslin for Star blocks

7½" x 13" piece of medium blue print for side setting triangles

15¾" x 15¾" piece of fabric for backing

6" x 16" piece of pink print for binding

14¾" x 14¾" piece of batting

CUTTING

All measurements include ¼"-wide seam allowances. Refer to "Cutting Bias Strips" on page 13.

From the red print, cut;
2 strips, each 1½" x 14", for Ninepatch blocks;
1 strip, 1½" x 8", for Ninepatch blocks;
2 squares, each 3" x 3", for corner setting triangles.

From yellow print #1, cut:
1 strip, 1½" x 14", for Ninepatch blocks.

From yellow print #2, cut:
2 strips, each 1½" x 8", for Ninepatch blocks.

From each of the 3 dark blue prints, stacked wrong sides up, cut:
2 bias strips, each 1½" x 15½", for Star blocks.

From the beige muslin, cut:
2 pieces, each 11" x 18", for Star blocks. Stack the pieces, right sides up, and cut from each piece:
3 bias strips, each 1½" x 15½", for Star blocks.
From the remainder, cut:
9 strips, each 1½" x 9", for Star blocks.

From the medium blue print, cut:
2 squares, each 5½" x 5½", for side setting triangles.

From the pink print, cut:
2 strips, each 1" x 12¾", for binding;
2 strips, each 1" x 14¾", for binding.

DIRECTIONS

Refer to "Quiltmaking Basics" on pages 11–33 for general instructions.

Piecing the Blocks

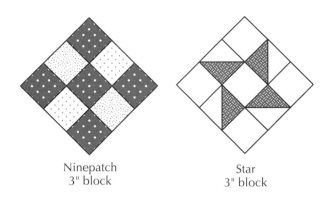

Ninepatch
3" block

Star
3" block

Press the seam allowances in the direction of the small arrows or as instructed.

NINEPATCH

1. Sew 2 red strips, each 1½" x 14", and 1 yellow strip, 1½" x 14", together to make 1 strip unit. Cut 8 segments, each 1½" wide.

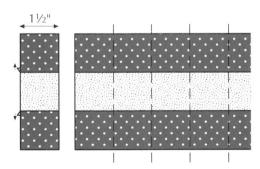

1½"

2. Sew 2 yellow strips, each 1½" x 8", and 1 red strip, 1½" x 8", together to make 1 strip unit. Cut 4 segments, each 1½" wide.

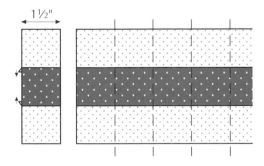

1½"

3. Sew the segments together to make 1 Ninepatch block. Make a total of 4 blocks.

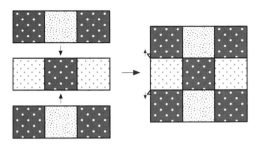

4. Press the blocks on both sides.

STAR

1. Sew a muslin bias strip to a dark blue bias strip to make 1 bias set. Make an additional bias set. Press the seams open.
2. With the wrong sides of the bias sets up, cut 6 bias squares, each 1½" x 1½", from each set for a total of 12 bias squares. Trim the seams to ⅛".
3. Stack the nine 1½" x 9" muslin strips and cut 5 squares, each 1½" x 1½", from each strip for a total of 45 squares.
4. Sew a 1½" muslin square to opposite edges of a bias square to make 1 unit. Make a total of 6 units.

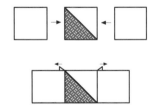

5. Sew a bias square to opposite edges of a 1½" muslin square to make 1 unit. Make a total of 3 units.

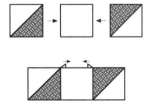

6. Sew the units together to make 1 Star block. Make a total of 3 matching blocks. Using the remaining assorted dark blue fabrics and muslin, make a total of 9 blocks.

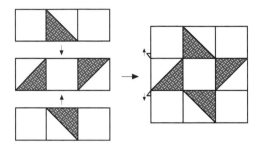

7. Press the blocks on both sides.
8. Stack the 5½" medium blue squares and cut in half twice diagonally for side setting triangles.

Assembling and Finishing the Quilt

1. Arrange the 13 pieced blocks and 8 side setting triangles into 5 diagonal rows. Join the blocks into rows. Press the triangle seams toward the triangles. Press the remaining seams toward the Ninepatch blocks.

2. Join the rows. Press the seams open or in the same direction.
3. Stack the 3" red squares and cut in half once diagonally for the corner setting triangles.
4. Sew the triangles to the quilt-top corners. Press the seams toward the triangles.

5. Press the quilt top on both sides and trim, if necessary.
6. Mark the top for quilting.
7. Layer the quilt top with batting and backing; baste. Quilt as desired.
8. Bind the edges with the 1"-wide pink strips.

Maple Leaf

Use the bias-square technique to piece the leaf stems and leaves in this quilt. The block construction is relatively simple; the challenge is in working with 1½" blocks.

❧

Finished Size: 10⅜" x 12½"

Finished Block Size: 1½" x 1½"

Color photo on page 35

Skill Level: Advanced

Techniques: Bias squares, quick-cut triangles, a diagonal setting, and one straight border with corner squares

MATERIALS: 44"-WIDE FABRIC

6" x 8" piece each of 12 assorted light prints for blocks

6" x 8" piece each of 12 assorted dark prints for blocks

9" x 12" piece of pink solid for plain squares and setting triangles

11" x 14" piece of purple print for borders and binding

9" x 11" piece of turquoise print for corner squares and binding

13⅜" x 15½" piece of fabric for backing

12⅜" x 14½" piece of batting

CUTTING

All measurements include ¼"-wide seam allowances. Refer to "Cutting Bias Strips" on page 13.

From the 12 assorted light prints, stacked wrong sides up, cut from each piece:
1 bias strip, 1" x 8½", for blocks;
2 bias strips, each 1" x 2", for blocks;
1 square, 1" x 1", for blocks.

From the 12 assorted dark prints, stacked right sides up, cut from each piece:
1 bias strip, 1" x 8½", for blocks;
1 bias strip, ⅝" x 2", for blocks;
1 rectangle, 1" x 1½", for blocks;
1 square, 1" x 1", for blocks.

From the pink solid, cut:
3 squares, each 3⅜" x 3⅜", for side setting triangles;
6 squares, each 2" x 2", for plain squares;
2 squares, each 2" x 2", for corner setting triangles.

From the purple print, cut:
2 strips, each 2¼" x 9", for border;
2 strips, each 2¼" x 6⅞", for border;
4 strips, each 1" x 2¼", for binding;
4 strips, each 1" x 3¼", for binding.

From the turquoise print, cut:
4 squares, each 2¼" x 2¼", for corner squares;
2 strips, each 1" x 9", for binding;
2 strips, each 1" x 6⅞", for binding.

DIRECTIONS

Refer to "Quiltmaking Basics" on pages 11–33 for general instructions.

Piecing the Blocks

Maple Leaf
1½" block

Press the seam allowances in the direction of the small arrows or as instructed.

1. Sew a 1" x 8½" light print bias strip to a 1" x 8½" dark print bias strip to make 1 bias set. Press the seam open.
2. With the wrong side of the bias set facing up, cut 4 bias squares, each 1" x 1". Trim the seams to ⅛".
3. Sew 2 bias squares together. Sew a matching 1" light print square to the left edge of the pieced unit. Trim the seams to ⅛".

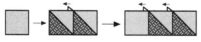

4. Sew a bias square to the left edge of a matching 1" x 1½" dark rectangle. Trim the seam to ⅛".

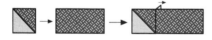

5. Sew the unit made in step 3 to the unit made in step 4, matching the seam. Trim the seam to ⅛".

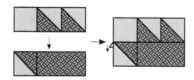

6. Sew a matching ⅝" x 2" dark print bias strip between two matching 1" x 2" light print bias strips to make 1 bias set. Press the seams toward the light strip. Trim the seams to ⅛".
7. Cut 1 bias square, 1" x 1", from the bias set.

8. Sew the bias square cut in step 2 to a matching 1" dark square. Sew the 1" bias square cut in step 7 to the right edge to make 1 unit. Trim the seams to ⅛".

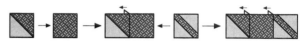

9. Sew the unit made in step 5 to the unit made in step 8, matching the seam, to complete 1 Maple Leaf block. Trim the seam to ⅛". Using the remaining assorted light and dark print fabrics, make a total of 12 scrap blocks.

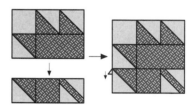

10. Press the blocks on both sides.
11. Stack 3 pink squares, each 3⅜", and cut in half twice diagonally for the side setting triangles. Set aside 2 triangles.

Assembling and Finishing the Quilt

1. Arrange the 12 pieced blocks, the six 2" pink squares, and 10 side setting triangles into 6 diagonal rows. Join the blocks into rows. Press the seams toward the plain squares and setting triangles.

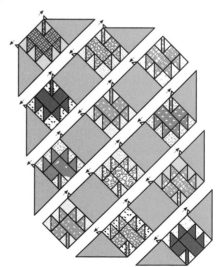

2. Join the rows. Press the seams open or in one direction. Trim the seams to ⅛".

3. Stack 2 pink squares, each 2", and cut in half once diagonally for the corner setting triangles.

4. Sew the triangles cut in step 3 to the quilt-top corners. Press the seams toward the triangles.

5. Sew the 2¼" x 9" purple border strips to the right and left edges of the quilt top. Press the seams toward the border.

6. Sew a 2¼" turquoise corner square to each end of the 2¼" x 6⅞" purple border strips to make 2 pieced border strips. Press the seams toward the border.

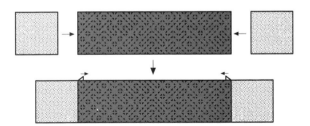

7. Sew the pieced border strips to the upper and lower edges of the quilt top, matching the seams. Press the seams toward the border.

8. Press the quilt top on both sides and trim, if necessary.

9. Mark the top for quilting.

10. Layer the quilt top with batting and backing; baste. Quilt as desired.

11. Sew a 1" x 2¼" purple binding strip to each end of the 1" x 9" turquoise binding strips to make 2 pieced binding strips. Press the seams toward the turquoise strips and trim to ⅛".

    Sew a 1" x 3¼" purple binding strip to each end of the 1" x 6⅞" turquoise binding strips to make 2 pieced binding strips. Press the seams toward the purple strips and trim to ⅛".

12. Sew the longer pieced binding strips to the right and left edges of the quilt, matching the corner-square seams. Fold the binding to the back of the quilt and blindstitch; see page 32.

    Repeat with the shorter pieced binding strips on the upper and lower edges.

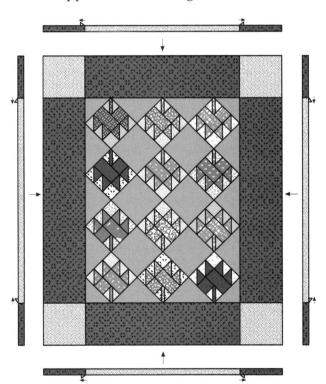

Sawtooth Flying Geese

The 3" scrap blocks are easy to assemble, but you must carefully match the points when you set the blocks side-by-side.

❧

Finished Size: 17½" x 17½"

Finished Block Size: 3" x 3"

Color photo on page 37

Skill Level: Intermediate

Techniques: Bias squares, quick-cut triangles, and two straight borders

MATERIALS: 44"-WIDE FABRIC

½ yd. white muslin for blocks and plain squares
½ fat quarter (11" x 18") each of 6 assorted dark blue prints for blocks
4" square each of 6 assorted red prints for blocks
6" x 15" piece of red print for inner border
1 fat quarter (18" x 22") of dark blue print for outer border and binding
20½" x 20½" piece of fabric for backing
19½" x 19½" piece of batting

CUTTING

All measurements include ¼"-wide seam allowances. Refer to "Cutting Bias Strips" on page 13.

From the muslin, cut:
3 pieces, each 11" x 18". Stack the pieces, wrong sides up, and cut from each piece:
  3 bias strips, each 1½" x 15½", for blocks.

From each of 3 leftover triangles, cut:
1 bias strip, 1½" x 15½", for blocks.
From the remainder, cut:
6 squares, each 2⅞" x 2⅞", for blocks;
4 squares, each 3½" x 3½", for plain squares.

From each of the 6 assorted dark blue prints, stacked right sides up, cut:
2 bias strips, each 1½" x 15½", for blocks.

From each of the 6 assorted red prints, cut:
1 square, each 2⅞" x 2⅞", for blocks.

From the 6" x 15" piece of red print, cut:
2 strips, each 1" x 12½", for inner border;
2 strips, each 1" x 13½", for inner border.

From the dark blue print, cut:
2 strips, each 2½" x 13½", for outer border;
2 strips, each 2½" x 17½", for outer border;
2 strips, each 1" x 17½", for binding;
2 strips, each 1" x 19½", for binding.

DIRECTIONS

Refer to "Quiltmaking Basics" on pages 11–33 for general instructions.

Piecing the Blocks

Sawtooth
3" block

Press the seam allowances in the direction of the small arrows or as instructed.

1. Sew a muslin bias strip to one of the assorted dark blue bias strips to make 1 bias set. Make an additional bias set. Press the seams open.

2. With the wrong sides of the bias sets facing up, cut 5 bias squares, each 1½" x 1½", from each set for a total of 10 bias squares. Trim the seams to ⅛".

3. Stack 6 muslin squares, each 2⅞", and cut in half once diagonally.

4. Stack 6 red print squares, each 2⅞", and cut in half once diagonally.

5. Sew 1 muslin triangle and 1 red triangle together to make 1 seamed square. Press the seam open and trim to ⅛". Trim the square to 2½", if necessary.

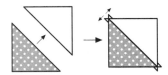

6. Sew 2 bias squares together. Sew this unit to the left edge of a seamed square made in step 5.

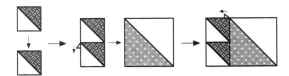

7. Sew 3 bias squares together. Sew this unit to the lower edge of the unit made in step 6, matching the seam, to complete 1 Sawtooth Flying Geese block. Using the remaining assorted print fabrics and muslin, make a total of 12 scrap blocks.

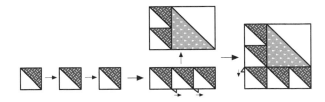

8. Press the blocks on both sides.

Assembling and Finishing the Quilt

1. Arrange the 12 pieced blocks and 4 muslin squares, each 3½", into 4 horizontal rows of 4 blocks each as shown in the quilt plan. Join the blocks into rows. Press the seams in opposite directions.

2. Join the rows. Press the seams in the same direction.

3. Sew the 1" x 12½" red border strips to the right and left edges of the quilt top. Press the seams toward the border and trim to ⅛". Repeat with the 1" x 13½" red border strips on the upper and lower edges.

4. Sew the 2½" x 13½" blue border strips to the right and left edges of the quilt top. Press the seams toward the border and trim to ⅛". Repeat with the 2½" x 17½" blue border strips on the upper and lower edges.

5. Press the quilt top on both sides and trim, if necessary.

6. Mark the top for quilting.

7. Layer the quilt top with batting and backing; baste. Quilt as desired.

8. Bind the edges with the 1"-wide dark blue strips.

Jacob's Ladder

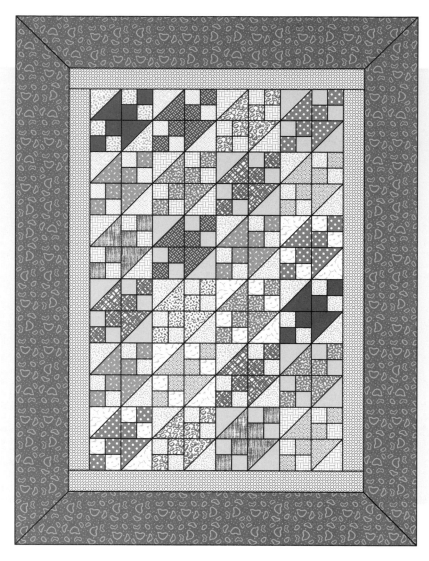

Because the pieces in this quilt are truly miniature, it's important to choose fabrics with good color contrast in a variety of prints. The side-by-side setting is relatively easy, and you need to match only one seam when joining the blocks.

❧

Finished Size: 10" x 11½"

Finished Block Size: 1½" x 1½"

Color photo on page 36

Skill Level: Advanced

Techniques: Bias squares, strip piecing, and straight and mitered borders

MATERIALS: 44"-WIDE FABRIC

4" x 9" piece each of 20 assorted dark prints for blocks
4" x 9" piece each of 20 assorted light prints for blocks
6" x 11" piece of dark green print for inner border
13" x 15" piece of dark blue print for outer border and binding
13" x 14½" piece of fabric for backing
12" x 13½" piece of batting

CUTTING

All measurements include ¼"-wide seam allowances. Refer to "Cutting Bias Strips" on page 13.

From each of the 20 assorted dark prints, stacked wrong sides up, cut:
1 bias strip, 1¼" x 4", for blocks;
1 strip, ⅞" x 5", for blocks.

From each of the 20 assorted light prints, stacked right sides up, cut:
1 bias strip, 1¼" x 4", for blocks;
1 strip, ⅞" x 5", for blocks.

From the dark green print, cut:
2 strips, each 1" x 9½", for inner border;
2 strips, each 1" x 7½", for inner border.

From the dark blue print, cut:
2 strips, each 1¾" x 14½", for outer border;
2 strips, each 1¾" x 13", for outer border;
2 strips, each 1" x 11½", for binding;
2 strips, each 1" x 12", for binding.

DIRECTIONS

Refer to "Quiltmaking Basics" on pages 11–33 for general instructions.

Piecing the Blocks

Jacob's Ladder
1½" block

Press the seam allowances in the direction of the small arrows or as instructed.

1. Sew a dark bias strip to a light bias strip to make 1 bias set. Press the seam open and trim to ⅛".
2. With the wrong side of the bias set facing up, cut 2 bias squares, each 1¼" x 1¼".
3. Sew a matching dark strip to a matching light strip, each ⅞" x 5", to make 1 unit. Press the seam open and trim to ⅛". Cut 4 segments, each ⅞" wide.

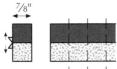

4. Sew 2 segments together, matching the seam, to make 1 Four Patch block. Make an additional block. Press the seams open and trim to ⅛".

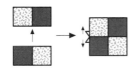

5. Press the blocks on both sides.
6. Sew a bias square to a Four Patch block to make 1 unit. Make an additional unit. Press the seams open and trim to ⅛".

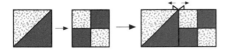

7. Sew the units together to complete 1 Jacob's Ladder block. Press the seams open and trim to ⅛". Using the remaining light and dark fabrics, make a total of 20 scrap blocks.

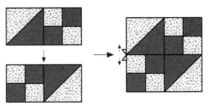

8. Press the blocks on both sides.

Assembling and Finishing the Quilt

1. Arrange the 20 pieced blocks in 5 horizontal rows of 4 blocks each as shown in the quilt plan. Join the blocks into rows, matching the seams. Press the seams in opposite directions and trim to ⅛".
2. Join the rows. Press the seams open or in the same direction.
3. Sew the 1" x 9½" green border strips to the right and left edges of the quilt top. Press the seams toward the border and trim to ⅛". Repeat with the 1" x 7½" green border strips on the upper and lower edges.
4. Referring to "Mitered Borders" on pages 27–28, sew the 1¾" x 14½" blue border strips to the right and left edges of the quilt top. Repeat with the 1¾" x 13" blue border strips on the upper and lower edges.
5. Press the quilt top on both sides and trim, if necessary.
6. Mark the top for quilting.
7. Layer the quilt top with batting and backing; baste. Quilt as desired.
8. Bind the edges with the 1"-wide blue strips.

Tennessee

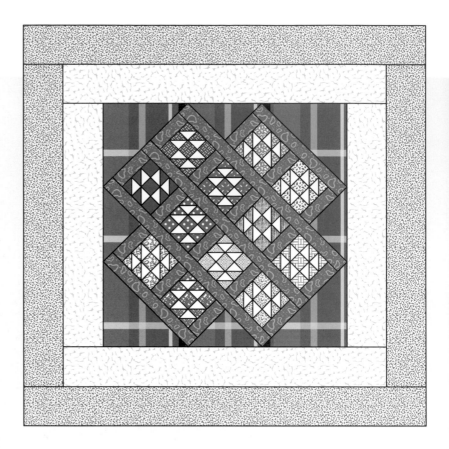

Narrow inner sashing separates the blocks from each other and makes them appear to float against a backdrop of setting triangles. Because the bias squares and sashing are so small, it's essential to cut and sew accurately.

❧

Finished Size: 15¾" x 15¾"

Finished Block Size: 1½" x 1½"

Color photo on page 38

Skill Level: Advanced

Techniques: Bias squares, quick-cut triangles, sashing, a diagonal setting, and two straight borders

MATERIALS: 44"-WIDE FABRIC

½ yd. light gold print for blocks
7¼" x 9" piece each of 12 assorted dark prints for blocks
9" x 12" piece of black print for sashing
10" x 20" piece of dark plaid for side and corner setting triangles and binding
10" x 15" piece of dark gold print for inner border
10" x 18" piece of medium green print for outer border
18¾" x 18¾" piece of fabric for backing
17¾" x 17¾" piece of batting

CUTTING

All measurements include ¼"-wide seam allowances. Refer to "Cutting Bias Strips" on page 13.

From the light gold print, cut:
6 pieces, each 7¼" x 9". Stack the pieces, wrong sides up, and cut from each piece:
   1 bias strip, 1" x 10", for blocks.

From each of 6 leftover triangles, cut:
   1 bias strip, 1" x 10", for blocks.

From the 12 assorted dark prints, stacked right sides up, cut from each piece:
1 bias strip, 1" x 10", for blocks;
3 squares, each 1" x 1", for blocks.

From the black print, cut:
16 strips, each 1" x 2", for vertical sashing;
2 strips, each 1" x 5", for horizontal sashing;
3 strips, each 1" x 9", for horizontal sashing.

From the dark plaid, cut:
1 square, 4⅛" x 4⅛", for side setting triangles;
2 squares, each 4" x 4", for corner setting triangles;
2 strips, each 1" x 15¾", for binding;
2 strips, each 1" x 17¾", for binding.

From the dark gold print, cut:
2 strips, each 2" x 9¾", for inner border;
2 strips, each 2" x 12¾", for inner border.

From the medium green print, cut:
2 strips, each 2" x 12¾", for outer border;
2 strips, each 2" x 15¾", for outer border.

DIRECTIONS

*Refer to "Quiltmaking Basics" on pages
11–33 for general instructions.*

Piecing the Blocks

Tennessee
1½" block

Press the seam allowances in the direction of the small arrows or as instructed.

1. Sew a light gold bias strip to a dark print bias strip to make 1 bias set. Press the seam open.
2. With the wrong side of the bias set facing up, cut 6 bias squares, each 1" x 1". Trim the seams to ⅛".
3. Sew 2 bias squares together. Sew a matching 1" dark print square to the right edge of the pair to make 1 unit. Make an additional unit. Press the seams open and trim to ⅛".

4. Sew a bias square to opposite edges of a 1" matching dark square to make 1 unit. Press the seams open and trim to ⅛".

5. Sew the units made in step 3 to the unit made in step 4, matching the seams, to complete 1 Tennessee block. Press the seams open and trim to ⅛". Using the remaining light and dark fabrics, make a total of 12 scrap blocks.

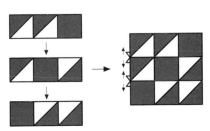

6. Press the blocks on both sides.
7. Arrange the blocks as shown below. Sew 16 black sashing strips, each 1" x 2", between the blocks and to the right and left edges to form rows. Press seams toward the sashing and trim to ⅛".

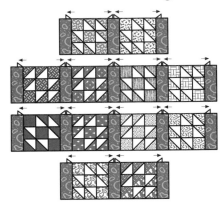

8. Sew the 2 black sashing strips, each 1" x 5", to the upper and lower rows. Press the seams toward the sashing and trim to ⅛".

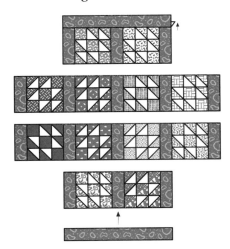

9. Cut the 4⅛" plaid square in half twice diagonally for the side setting triangles. Sew the triangles to the right and left edges of the upper and lower rows. Press the seams toward the triangles.

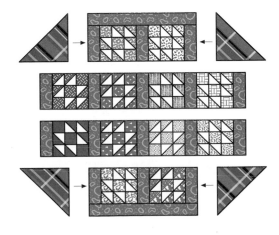

10. Sew the 3 black horizontal sashing strips, each 1" x 9", between the rows. Press the seams toward the sashing and trim to ⅛".

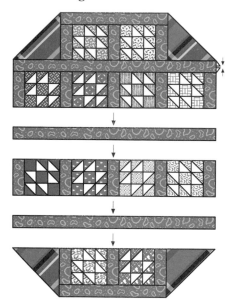

11. Stack the 2 plaid squares, each 4", and cut in half once diagonally for the corner setting triangles. Sew the triangles to the quilt-top corners. Press the seams toward the triangles.

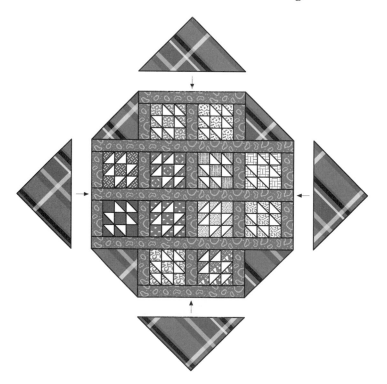

Assembling and Finishing the Quilt

1. Sew the 2" x 9¾" dark gold border strips to the right and left edges of the quilt top. Press the seams toward the border. Repeat with the 2" x 12¾" dark gold border strips on the upper and lower edges.

2. Sew the 2" x 12¾" green border strips to the right and left edges of the quilt top. Press the seams toward the border. Repeat with the 2" x 15¾" green border strips on the upper and lower edges.

3. Press the quilt top on both sides and trim, if necessary.

4. Mark the top for quilting.

5. Layer the quilt top with batting and backing; baste. Quilt as desired.

6. Bind the edges with the 1"-wide plaid strips.

Fish School

This jaunty quilt features two easy-to-assemble Fish blocks and two Boat blocks as corner squares, which are more challenging to make. Larger setting triangles make the Fish blocks float.

❧

Finished Size: 12⅞" x 15"

Finished Block Sizes: 1½" and 2"

Color photo on page 34

Skill Level: Advanced

Techniques: Bias squares, quick-cut triangles, floating blocks, and two straight borders

MATERIALS: 44"-WIDE FABRIC

1 fat quarter (18" x 22") of light turquoise print for Fish blocks

6" x 9" piece each of 10 assorted prints for Fish blocks

6" x 9" piece each of 2 different prints for Fish blocks

11" x 15" piece of dark turquoise print for plain squares and side and corner setting triangles

6" x 12" piece of orange print for inner border

7" x 10" piece of light green print for Boat blocks

7" x 10" piece of red-and-white stripe for Boat blocks

3" x 5" piece of red-and-navy blue check for Boat blocks

5" x 6" piece of green-and-white print for Boat blocks

3½" x 6" piece of blue print for Boat blocks

3" x 5" piece of pink plaid for Boat blocks

12" x 13" piece of multicolored turquoise print for outer border

15⅞" x 18" piece of fabric for backing

6" x 17" piece of purple print for binding

14⅞" x 17" piece of batting

CUTTING

All measurements include ¼"-wide seam allowances. Refer to "Cutting Bias Strips" on page 13.

From the light turquoise print, cut:

3 pieces, each 6" x 14". Stack the pieces, wrong sides up, and cut from each piece:

3 bias strips, each 1¼" x 8½", for Fish block A.

From 1 leftover triangle, cut:

1 bias strip, 1¼" x 8½", for Fish block A.

From each of 2 leftover triangles, cut:

1 bias strip, 1" x 8½", for Fish block B;

2 squares, each 1⅜" x 1⅜", for Fish block B.

From each of the 10 assorted prints, stacked right sides up, cut:

1 bias strip, 1¼" x 8½", for Fish block A.

From each of the 2 different prints, stacked right sides up, cut:

1 bias strip, 1" x 8½", for Fish block B.

From the remainder, cut:

1 square, 1⅜" x 1⅜", for Fish block B;

1 square, 2⅜" x 2⅜", for Fish block B.

From the dark turquoise print, cut:

3 squares, each 4¼" x 4¼", for side setting triangles;

6 squares, each 2" x 2", for plain squares;

2 squares, each 2¾" x 2¾", for corner setting triangles.

From the orange print, cut:

2 strips, each 1" x 10", for inner border;

2 strips, each 1" x 8⅞", for inner border.

From the light green print, wrong side up, cut:

1 bias strip, 1½" x 10", for Boat block A.

From the 2 leftover triangles, cut:

1 bias strip, 1¼" x 5", for Boat block B;

2 strips, each ¾" x 1¼", for Boat block B;

2 strips, each 1" x 1½", for Boat block B;

2 strips, each 1¼" x 1½", for Boat block B;

4 squares, each 1⅜" x 1⅜", for Boat blocks A and B.

From the red-and-white stripe, right side up, cut:

1 bias strip, 1½" x 10", for Boat block A.

From the red-and-navy blue check, cut:

2 strips, each 1" x 3¼", for Boat block A.

From the green-and-white print, cut:

4 strips, each 1" x 2½", for Boat blocks A and B.

From the blue print, right side up, cut:

1 bias strip, 1¼" x 5", for Boat block B.

From the pink plaid, cut:

2 strips, each 1" x 3¼", for Boat block B.

From the multicolored turquoise print, cut:

2 strips, each 2½" x 11", for outer border;

2 strips, each 2½" x 8⅞", for outer border.

From the purple print, cut:

2 strips, each 1" x 15", for binding;

2 strips, each 1" x 14⅞", for binding.

DIRECTIONS

Refer to "Quiltmaking Basics" on pages 11–33 for general instructions.

Piecing the Blocks

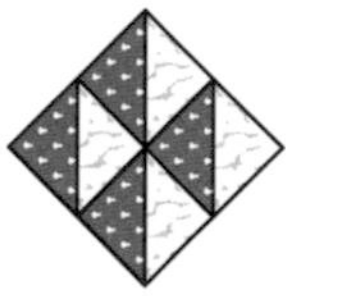

Fish Block A
1½" block

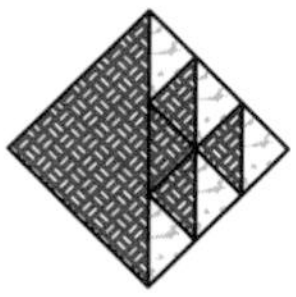

Fish Block B
1½" block

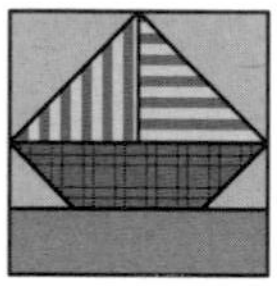

Boat Block A
2" block

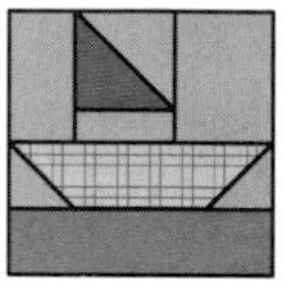

Boat Block B
2" block

Press the seam allowances in the direction of the small arrows or as instructed.

FISH BLOCK A

1. Sew a light turquoise 1¼" x 8½" bias strip to 1 of the 10 assorted 1¼" x 8½" print bias strips to make 1 bias set. Press the seam open.
2. With the wrong side of the bias set facing up, cut 4 bias squares, each 1¼" x 1¼". Trim the seams to ⅛".
3. Sew 2 bias squares together to make 1 unit. Press the seam open and trim to ⅛". Make an additional unit.

4. Sew the units together, matching the center seam, to complete 1 Fish block A. Press the seam open and trim to ⅛". Using the remaining turquoise and print fabrics, make a total of 10 blocks.

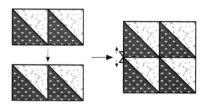

5. Press the blocks on both sides.

FISH BLOCK B

1. Sew a light turquoise 1" x 8½" bias strip to 1 of the 2 different 1" x 8½" print bias strips to make 1 bias set. Press the seam open.

2. With the wrong side of the bias set facing up, cut 3 bias squares, each 1" x 1". Trim the seams to ⅛".

3. Cut one 1⅜" light turquoise square in half once diagonally.

4. Sew 2 bias squares together. Sew a triangle cut in step 3 to the left edge. Press the seams open and trim to ⅛".

5. Cut one 1⅜" print square in half once diagonally. Set aside 1 triangle.

6. Sew a print triangle cut in step 5 to a bias square. Press the seam open and trim to ⅛".

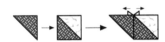

7. Sew the unit made in step 4 to the unit made in step 6, matching the seam. Press the seam open and trim to ⅛".

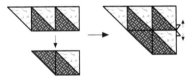

8. Sew a light turquoise triangle cut in step 3 to the lower edge of the unit made in step 7. Press the seam open and trim to ⅛".

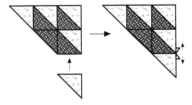

9. Cut one 2⅜" print square in half once diagonally. Set aside 1 triangle.

10. Sew the triangle cut in step 9 to the unit made in step 8 to complete 1 Fish block B. Press the seam open and trim to ⅛". Using the remaining light turquoise and print fabrics, make an additional block.

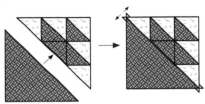

11. Press the blocks on both sides.

Assembling the Fish Blocks

1. Stack the 3 dark turquoise squares, each 4¼", and cut in half twice diagonally for the side setting triangles. Set aside 2 triangles.

2. Arrange the 12 pieced Fish blocks, six 2" dark turquoise squares, and 10 side setting triangles into 6 diagonal rows. Join the blocks into rows. Press the seams toward the plain squares and setting triangles.

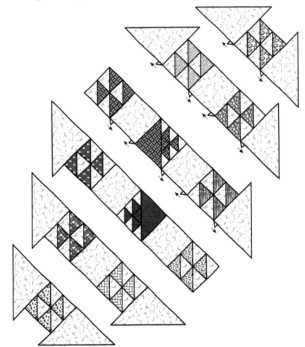

3. Join the rows. Press the seams open or in the same direction.
4. Stack the 2 dark turquoise squares, each 2¾", and cut in half once diagonally for the corner setting triangles.
5. Sew the triangles to the quilt-top corners. Press the seams toward the triangles.

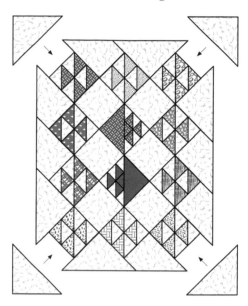

6. Barely trim the edges of the quilt top. Maintain ¼"-wide seam allowances and leave enough fabric so the blocks will float.
7. Sew the 1" x 10" orange border strips to the right and left edges of the quilt top. Press the seams toward the border and trim to ⅛". Repeat with the 1" x 8⅞" orange border strips on the upper and lower edges.

BOAT BLOCK A

1. Sew a light green bias strip, 1½" x 10", to a red-and-white stripe bias strip, 1½" x 10", to make 1 bias set. Press the seam open.
2. With the wrong side of the bias set facing up, cut 4 bias squares, each 1½" x 1½". Press the seams open and trim to ⅛".
3. Sew 2 bias squares together to make 1 unit. Make an additional unit. Press the seams open and trim to ⅛".

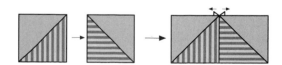

4. Stack 2 red-and-navy blue check rectangles, each 1" x 3¼"; trim the corners at a 45° angle.

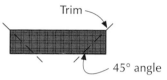

5. Stack 2 light green squares, each 1⅜", and cut in half once diagonally.
6. Sew a triangle cut in step 5 to each end of a rectangle trimmed in step 4 to make 1 unit. Make an additional unit. Press the seams open and trim to ⅛".

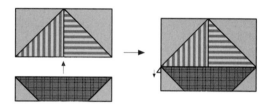

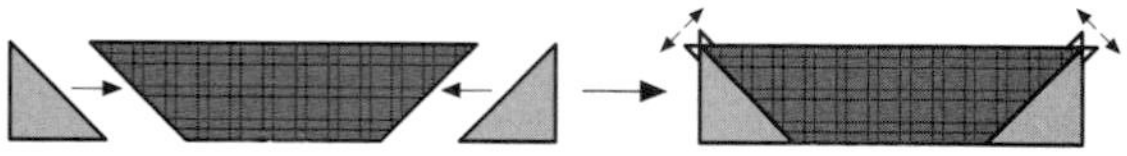

7. Sew the unit made in step 6 to the unit made in step 3, matching the seams. Make an additional unit. Trim the seams to ⅛".

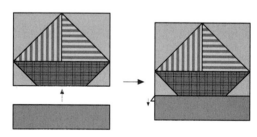

8. Sew a green-and-white rectangle, 1" x 2½", to the unit made in step 7 to complete 1 Boat block A. Make an additional Boat block. Trim the seams to ⅛".

9. Press the blocks on both sides.

BOAT BLOCK B

1. Sew a light green bias strip, 1¼" x 5", to a blue bias strip, 1¼" x 5", to make 1 bias set. Press the seam open.
2. With the wrong side of the bias set facing up, cut 2 bias squares, each 1¼" x 1¼". Trim the seams to ⅛".

3. Sew 1 light green rectangle, ¾" x 1¼", to the lower edge of the bias square to make 1 unit. Make an additional unit. Trim the seams to ⅛".

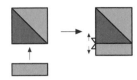

4. Sew 1 light green rectangle, 1" x 1½", to the left edge of the unit made in step 3. Make an additional unit. Trim the seam to ⅛".

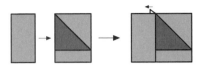

5. Sew 1 light green rectangle, 1¼" x 1½", to the right edge of the unit made in step 4. Make an additional unit. Trim the seams to ⅛".

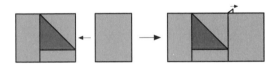

6. Stack 2 pink plaid rectangles, each 1" x 3¼", and trim the corners at a 45° angle.
7. Stack 2 light green squares, each 1⅜", and cut in half once diagonally.
8. Sew a triangle cut in step 7 to each end of a rectangle trimmed in step 6. Make an additional unit. Press the seams open and trim to ⅛".
9. Sew the unit made in step 8 to the unit made in step 5. Make an additional unit.

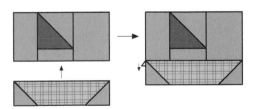

10. Sew a green-and-white rectangle, 1" x 2½", to the lower edge of the unit made in step 9 to complete 1 Boat block B. Complete the second block. Trim the seams to ⅛".

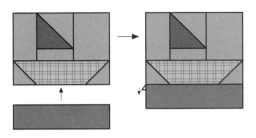

11. Press the blocks on both sides.

Assembling and Finishing the Quilt

1. Sew the 2½" x 11" multicolored border strips to the right and left edges of the quilt top. Press the seams toward the border.
2. Sew a different Boat block to each end of a 2½" x 8⅞" multicolored border strip. Press the seams toward the border. Make an additional pieced border strip, reversing the position of the Boat blocks.

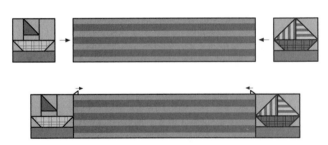

3. Sew the pieced border strips to the upper and lower edges of the quilt top, matching corner-square seams. Press the seams toward the border.
4. Press the quilt top on both sides and trim, if necessary.
5. Mark the top for quilting.
6. Layer the quilt top with batting and backing; baste. Quilt as desired.
7. Bind the edges with the 1"-wide purple strips.

Bibliography

Berg, Alice, Sylvia Johnson, and Mary Ellen Von Holt. *Little Quilts.* Bothell, Wash.: That Patchwork Place, 1993.

Goldberg, Rhoda Ochser. *The New Quilting and Patchwork Dictionary.* New York: Crown Publishers, Inc., 1988.

Hickey, Mary. *Little by Little: Quilts in Miniature.* Bothell, Wash.: That Patchwork Place, 1988.

Horton, Roberta. *Plaids and Stripes: The Use of Directional Fabric in Quilts.* Lafayette, Calif.: C & T Publishing, 1990.

Imbach, Gay. *Miniature Magic: 150 Patchwork Patterns.* Corona, Calif.: Imbach Publications, 1981.

Marston, Gwen, and Joe Cunningham. *Twenty Little Patchwork Quilts with Full-Size Templates.* New York, N.Y.: Dover Publications, Inc., 1990.

McClun, Diana, and Laura Nownes. *Quilts!, Quilts!!, Quilts!!!: The Complete Guide to Quiltmaking.* San Francisco: The Quilt Digest Press, 1988.

McKelvey, Susan Richardson. *Color for Quilters.* Westminster, Calif.: A Yours Truly Publication, 1984.

Nephew, Sara. *My Mother's Quilts: Designs from the Thirties.* Bothell, Wash.: That Patchwork Place, 1988.

Schaefer, Becky. *Working in Miniature: A Machine Piecing Approach to Miniature Quilts.* Lafayette, Calif.: C & T Publishing, 1987.

Thomas, Debra Lynn. *Small Talk.* Bothell, Wash.: That Patchwork Place, 1991.

Voudrie, Sylvia Trygg. *Tiny Traditions.* Montrose, Pa.: Chitra Publications, 1992.

Woodard, Thomas, and Mimi Greenstein. *Crib Quilts and Other Small Wonders.* New York: Bonanza Books, 1988.

Zimmerman, Darlene. *Companions, Quilts and Miniatures.* Saddle Brook, N.J.: EZ International, 1992.

Meet the Author

Christine Carlson joined the quilt world ten years ago and has been an avid miniature-quilt maker ever since. She made her first small quilts on a whim, using tiny sandpaper templates and piecing by hand. Once she discovered rotary cutting, her quilting life changed forever. Now, she says, she can't begin to stitch all the miniature quilts she wants to make.

Christine strives for perfection in her work and encourages her students to have "P and P" (patience and perseverance) when making miniatures—so there's less need to "R and R" (rip and resew)! Over the years, she has taught a variety of techniques for making miniatures, including paper foundation piecing, strip piecing, and bias squares. The versatility and ease of the Bias Square technique inspired her to write *Bias Square Miniatures.*

In addition to making miniature quilts, Christine collects antique fabrics and quilt tops. She is particularly fond of the bright colors and unusual prints from the 1930s and 1940s. If a quilt top is in poor condition and the pieces are large enough, she uses the vintage fabrics to make one-of-a-kind, scrappy miniatures.

Christine lives in Norcross, Georgia. She teaches and lectures regionally, and writes articles for miniature-quilt magazines.